Open access edition supported by the National Endowment for the Humanities /
Andrew W. Mellon Foundation Humanities Open Book Program.

© 2019 Johns Hopkins University Press
Published 2019

Johns Hopkins University Press
2715 North Charles Street
Baltimore, Maryland 21218-4363
www.press.jhu.edu

ISBN-13: 978-1-4214-3681-4 (open access)
ISBN-10: 1-4214-3681-7 (open access)

ISBN-13: 978-1-4214-3679-1 (pbk. : alk. paper)
ISBN-10: 1-4214-3679-5 (pbk. : alk. paper)

ISBN-13: 978-1-4214-3680-7 (electronic)
ISBN-10: 1-4214-3680-9 (electronic)

This page supersedes the copyright page included in the original publication of this work.

EUROPEAN LANDED ELITES
IN THE NINETEETH CENTURY

THE JOHNS HOPKINS SYMPOSIA
IN COMPARATIVE HISTORY

The Johns Hopkins Symposia in Comparative History are occasional volumes, sponsored by the Department of History at The Johns Hopkins University and The Johns Hopkins University Press, by leading scholars in the United States and other countries. Each essay considers, from a comparative perspective, an important topic of current historical interest. The present volume is the eighth. Its preparation has been assisted by the James S. Schouler Lecture Fund.

EUROPEAN LANDED ELITES IN THE NINETEENTH CENTURY

Edited and with an
introductory chapter by

David Spring

THE JOHNS HOPKINS UNIVERSITY PRESS
Baltimore and London

Manufactured in the United States of America

The Johns Hopkins University Press, Baltimore, Maryland 21218
The Johns Hopkins Press Ltd., London

Library of Congress Catalog Card Number: 77–4549
ISBN: 0–8018–1953–9

Library of Congress Cataloging in Publication data
will be found on the last printed page of this book.

Contents

Acknowledgments

For invaluable help on the subject of entail and inheritance law, I am indebted to my wife, Eileen. For sundry information and advice, I am indebted to Jerome Blum, Richard Herr, and Michael Thompson, among the contributors to the volume; to Mack Walker, colleague at The Johns Hopkins University; and to Lamar Cecil, Frederick Gillen, Edward Malefakis, and James Sheehan of the University of North Carolina, the State University of New York, Columbia University, and Northwestern University, respectively.

David Spring

DAVID SPRING

1 | Landed Elites Compared

Apart from what has been written on the English landed elite, not a great deal has been written on the history of European landed elites in the nineteenth century. Still less has been written in a comparative vein. There is nothing for the nineteenth century comparable to the series of essays on the eighteenth-century aristocracies edited by Albert Goodwin.[1] There is, of course, Barrington Moore's *Social Origins of Dictatorship and Democracy*, a remarkable and pertinent work, but even this does not dwell much on the nineteenth century.[2]

It was timely therefore that the Schouler Lectures at The Johns Hopkins University in 1974 should have taken as their topic the history of European landed elites in the nineteenth century. Specialists, each well known in his field, lectured in turn on the English, Prussian, Russian, Spanish, and French landed elites. Each lecturer was asked to address himself to the problem of how his particular landed elite coped with the difficulties of the nineteenth century; how it accommodated itself to the aspirations of new elites; how, in short, it managed to survive as well or as badly as it did. As might be expected, the lecturers differed in their preoccupations—one being an economic historian, for example, another a political historian. The lectures therefore differed in their emphasis. Nonetheless, each provided an enlightening account of landed vicissitudes, and together they marked an advance in the study of European landed elites. In this volume the lectures are made available to a wider audience. Since the lecturers were not asked to deal in systematic comparisons, comparing the landed elites has fallen to my lot in this introduction.

Historians sometimes show a fondness for an ambitious sort of comparative history—one that is drastically sociological and that strenuously explains with the aid of typologies, schedules of fundamental causes, and high-level generalizations. It is as well to be clear at the outset that I do not aspire to this. There is a more modest sort of

1

comparative history, one that explains by dwelling on differences. It seeks, as Marc Bloch put it, "to analyse and isolate the 'originality' of different societies."[3] It is this sort of comparative history that I have in mind here. Since I know most about the English landed elite I will inevitably come down most heavily on its peculiarities. Original research of a serious sort on Continental landed elites is of course beyond me. If no more comes, however, of this essay in comparative history than asking questions and finding where we are ignorant, it should be of use.

This introduction will fall into two main parts. The first, largely economic and legal, will discuss several fundamental matters: the pattern of landownership, inheritance laws and customs, habits of residence, and estate management. The second part will discuss political power and collective mentality.

I

Useful discussion of patterns of landownership obviously requires statistical information. This is not, however, always easily come by, and sometimes even when it is plentiful it does not lend itself to enlightening comparisons. Nineteenth-century Spain, for example, produced few landed statistics of any sort. Nineteenth-century France, usually prolific in the production of statistics, supplied much on agricultural subjects but almost nothing on the subject of landownership. Nineteenth-century Prussia was more forthcoming about its landowners, but its statistics have their limitations and can mislead the unwary, as indeed can the French.[4] In short, although rightly given large importance in recent years, quantification has its frustrations, which a comparative context renders all the more severe. Nevertheless, enough statistics are available to let some light into a hitherto obscure subject.

England possesses what is the most thorough survey in the nineteenth century of a nation's landowning structure. Over the period 1874–6 the government published, in what is generally known as the New Domesday Book, the results of a special census identifying landowners and indicating the location and size of their estates.[5] Before 1874 critics of the English estate system had charged that there were no more than 30,000 owners. Although the New Domesday Book turned up about a million, it also revealed that about 80 percent of the land of the United Kingdom was owned by some 7,000 persons.

For England (as distinct from the United Kingdom), the New Domesday Book showed that 25 percent of the land was in the hands of 363 landowners, usually titled, who held estates of 10,000 acres and more. Another 30 percent was in the hands of 3,000 owners, usually untitled gentry, who held estates ranging from 1,000 to 10,000 acres. In nineteenth-century England something like 1,000 acres was the minimum estate size for members of the landed elite.[6] Altogether then, the English landed elite owned at least 55 percent of English land. Owners of estates from 300 to 1,000 acres numbered about 10,000 and held about 14 percent, and those owning estates of 100 to 300 acres held about 12 percent. Public bodies, that is, the crown, church, government departments, and educational institutions, owned a mere 3 percent of English land.[7]

Dr Zeldin suggests that French landed estates were smaller on the whole than English. He points out that France had no leviathan like the 80,000-acred duke of Bedford and that even estates of 10,000 acres were remarkable. He also points out that French official statistics have little to say on the subject of landownership: they count not owners but what the *enquête agricole* of 1882 called *exploitations*,[8] that is to say, farming units. Some students of the subject—mistaking these farming units for ownership units and convinced that the French landed elite was a poor thing—have leapt on the official statistic for 1882 of 921 *exploitations* above 1,000 acres to prove their point.[9] In effect they would have it that although England was about one-quarter the size of France it could boast of 3,360 landowners with estates over 1,000 acres owning together 55 percent of the land, whereas France had only 921 owners of this size owning 1 percent of French land. The French landed elite may have been a poor thing, but it was not this poor.

Is there anything to be said on this matter that is at once precise and reliable? If we assume that the French landed elite was more or less equivalent in the eighteenth century to the French nobility, then we may use for a start Pierre Goubert's recent assessment that the pre-revolutionary nobility owned 25 percent of the land of France.[10] Authorities, to be sure, have disagreed about what happened to French estates during the Revolution, but not, it would seem, substantially. In the nineteenth century the agronomist Lavergne argued, somewhat arbitrarily, that over the long run the landed elite lost very little.[11] A modern historian, after careful research, has concluded that in the Toulouse region noble estates diminished in size about 20 percent.[12] If the Toulouse figure is representative, then the Revolution was not of much consequence: holding about 25 percent in the eighteenth century, the landed elite in the early nineteenth century held about 20 percent of the land of France.

This not too unreliable estimate is to be set against the solid 55 percent held by the English landed elite. The latter figure would rise to 69 percent if elite status in England were attached to estates from 300 to 1,000 acres as was the case in France and elsewhere on the Continent.[13] All this, of course, tells us nothing about the number of French landowners or about the range in size of their estates. As noted earlier, however, large French estates were not as conspicuous as the English—an impression shared by that inveterate worshipper of aristocracies, Benjamin Disraeli, who chose to scorn the French: "Where are their territories? [he sneered] . . . Henry Hope and de Rothschild could buy them all."[14]

In at least one important respect—in the proportion of the national territory owned—the pattern of Prussian landownership was more like the English than the French. Prussian landowners with estates of 375 acres and more—which Prussian statisticians in the 1850s defined as large estates and which contemporaries regarded as elite estates— numbered about 15,000, in a country that was about twice the size of England. In aggregate these Prussian landowners held about 40 percent of the land of Prussia in 1858, a proportion that increased in prime Junker provinces such as Pomerania and Posen to 62 percent and 57 percent respectively.[15] Although it does not seem possible to be precise about the number of estates over 10,000 acres, evidence suggests that they were less numerous than English estates of that size. In short, the Prussian landed elite was a more homogeneous body than the English.[16]

Prussian statistics, like the French, need a word of caution. They provide certain figures on what are called *Rittergüter*, that is, "privileged" estates, or manorial jurisdictions.[17] These figures show that among some 12,000 *Rittergüter* from 1835 to 1864 there were 14,400 sales, 1,300 foreclosures, and 7,900 hereditary transmissions. Historians considering these figures have said that they show "a two-hundred percent turnover in the ownership of some 12,000 large estates in the eastern provinces," and that each estate "changed hands on average more than twice (2.14 times) during these thirty years."[18] These are misleading statements if, as would seem to be their purport, they are intended to suggest an unusual measure of social mobility, to indicate a marked weakening of traditional landed power in Prussia. First, they include hereditary transmissions with sales; but hereditary transmissions are logically to be contrasted with sales, not lumped with them. Moreover, even if sales are considered separately, what is implied is uncertain. The figures tell nothing about the nature of the sales. How many of them, for example, were sales from small to large landowners, that is, were transfers within the landowning class? Finally, while the figures do show what at first sight seems a high ratio of sales to hereditary transmissions, there is no certainty even of this. *Rittergüter* were small estates, many of them very small: of the 12,000, more than 7,000 were 100 to 400 acres in size. Small estates in all land markets, even aristocratic ones, tend to change hands with some frequency without seriously altering the balance of traditional landed power.[19] In short, to use *Rittergüter* statistics to suggest a large-scale turnover in the ownership of Prussian estates is a dubious enterprise.[20]

When asked in the 1860s to report to his government on the subject of Spanish landownership, the First Secretary of the British legation in Madrid threw up his hands in despair: there was, he wrote, an "absence of printed statistics and immense difficulty of procuring any information which is not purely local."[21] This was not an example of bureaucratic indolence, but was the simple truth. The First Secretary would, moreover, have had to wait a long time—until well into the twentieth century—for the supply of Spanish statistics to improve. The following statistics are thus not directly relevant to Spanish landholding in the nineteenth century, but they may suggest a rough order of magnitude. In a national territory much like that of France in size, or about four times that of England, large estates ("large" meaning above 250 acres) numbered about 50,000 and accounted for 52 percent of Spanish land. More than half of these estates were in southern Spain, the home of the Spanish *latifundium*. Great estates (those over 12,500 acres) numbered 344.[22]

Professor Blum's table on Russian landholding provides much interesting information. Nobility went cheaply in Russia: it was a personal status, so to speak, and often had little to do with the possession of land. In 1877 some 55,000 Russian nobles each owned less than 100 desiatins of land (270 acres), the amount considered necessary to landed status. Many nobles of course did possess landed status—about 57,000 of them. Of this number, some 44,000 held estates between 100 and 1,000 desiatins, and some 13,000 held estates over 1,000 desiatins. About 150 nobles owned estates over 135,000 acres. Some in the last group owned vast principalities. The Sheremetev family, probably the greatest of Russian landowners, at the end of the eighteenth century owned almost 3 million acres, which a half century later had fallen to a mere 2 million.[23]

These huge figures tend to make the mind boggle; but put in a comparative perspective, they are much less impressive. European Russia was a huge area, roughly 1,200 million acres, or about ten times the size of France.[24] Russian noble landowners owned altogether in 1877 about 177 million acres, or something like 14 percent of the territory of European Russia. This would put the Russian elite, measured in terms of its ownership of national territory, in the same class as the French elite. The Russian elite owed its relatively weak position to two facts: first, the Russian peasantry held 116 million desiatins of European Russia as compared to the elite's 73 million; and second, the state towered over both the peasantry and the nobility, owning 166 million desiatins. There was nothing in the West comparable to the Russian state's vast preponderance in Russian land-ownership.

To sum up: no Continental landed elite in the nineteenth century owned so large a part of its nation's territory as did the English. The Spanish landed elite, for whom we have only twentieth-century statistics, was possibly its closest rival. Next came the Prussian, with the French and Russian lagging far behind. Not only did the English landed elite own a major part of the land of England but it also had no competitors in the countryside. No land-hungry peasantry faced it, as was the case in France, Spain, and Russia, nor did a land-wealthy State tower over it, as was the case in Russia. If the undisputed possession of much land was a measure of power, the English landed elite was indeed powerful.

Inheritance laws and customs also varied. Each country had developed some form of entail, that primal aristocratic device for preserving estates intact from generation to generation. In Prussia and Russia, as in prerevolutionary France, there was the *fideicommissum*; in postrevolutionary France there was the *majorat*; in Spain, the *mayorazgo*; and in England, the strict family settlement. Entails, however, were to have different histories from country to country in the nineteenth century, largely as a result of modern economic forces and antiaristocratic sentiment.

In England landowners possessed in the strict family settlement a unique form of entail, and one that was to continue in its essentials unchanged for nearly all the century. It was not a true entail, that is, it was not perpetual, for perpetuities were outlawed in England before the end of the fifteenth century. Settlement was all the better for that. It was a limited entail that struck a nice balance between mortmain and free alienation.[25] It managed, as so many things English seem to have done, to get the best of two worlds. On the one hand, it passed estates intact—except for relatively small mortgages for younger children's portions—from father to eldest son generation after generation.

Each possessed the estate only as a tenant for life and was therefore incapable of selling it or dealing with it according to whim. On the other hand, strict family settlements were to a degree flexible. Not being perpetual, they required renegotiation from time to time, usually each generation between father and son. This flexibility was increased in the nineteenth century both by private custom and by statute law so that estate development might not be frustrated by legal rigidities. Most landowners in England practised settlement, and the amount of English land in settlement was high. Estimates vary, but an authoritative one is that settlement covered 50 percent of English land.[26]

English landowners were blessed not only in the strict family settlement but also in other provisions of the law. Where a landowner held land absolutely—either through purchase or because part of his estate was out of settlement or through the accidents inescapable in a limited form of entail—he was free to will it as he chose. He was never limited by rules requiring him to divide his property. He could thus prefer his eldest son to any degree. Should he die intestate—though this was unlikely—aristocratic principles prevailed. The law divided his personal property among his children, but it gave his land wholly to his eldest son.

In France in the nineteenth century the laws were not conducive to the preservation of estates. Even before the Revolution, it is worth mentioning, French landowners lived in a less congenial legal atmosphere than did their English counterparts. France, unlike England, had to bear in mind the landed interests of a numerous peasantry. Accordingly, the inheritance laws of the *ancien régime* seemed, by English ideas, to be at cross-purposes. On the one hand, French law did not object to perpetuities, and perpetual entails were legal. On the other hand, the law showed a disposition to divide property—including landed property—among children. This disposition varied in strength according to the social class of the owner, but it was never absent. Thus upon intestacy, which was normal to peasants, Roman law divided property equally among children; so too did the customary laws of many provinces. Even in testamentary dispositions division among children was required, although by no means equal division. The testator could freely dispose of anywhere from three-quarters to one-half of his property, and the aspiring could therefore favor their eldest sons.[27] On noble estates primogeniture and entail prevailed. It was, however, a limited primogeniture, the law guaranteeing a portion—usually one-third—to the younger children. How this all worked out on prerevolutionary landed estates we do not know with any certainty. The evidence we have suggests, what would seem reasonable, that French landowners had less of their land in entail and made larger provisions for younger children than did English landowners.[28]

The Revolution, of course, put an end to both primogeniture and entail. Moreover, under the Convention all testamentary freedom disappeared. Compulsory equal division became the rule. The Napoleonic Civil Code soon moderated this rule, allowing the favoring of one child to a limited extent. Where there were four children, for example, one might receive two-fifths of the estate.[29] In sum, however, fragmentation came in the nineteenth century to haunt the French landed estate. It did so even though Napoleon in 1808, in an effort to found a new nobility for his new throne, reinstituted entail in the form of the *majorat*. In theory perpetual, *majorats* in fact were ephemeral. Since the founder of a *majorat* had still to make provision for his younger children in accordance with the inheritance law, *majorats* tended to be small.[30] They were also few. Only 440 were created before the Revolution of 1830.[31] Five years later further creations were forbidden, and by 1849 those already established were practically abolished.[32]

Spanish law in the nineteenth century followed a course generally similar to that of France. Entails were abolished and compulsory division became the rule of inheritance. Accordingly Spanish landowners like the French faced the problem of fragmentation. There were, however, differences between the two countries that go some way to explaining the greater success of the Spanish in overcoming it. First, entails existed longer in Spain, being abolished in 1836. Second, the Spanish law compelling the division of property allowed for the greater favoring of one child. One child in a family of four might receive three-quarters of the property.[33] Finally, it is arguable, as Professor Herr does in his paper, that Spanish landowners augmented their estates upon the abolition of entail through buying church lands, for these were not only disentailed but forcibly sold. Lay landowners would thus have counteracted for a while the tendency to fragmentation which the disentail of their own lands involved.

Prussia, like England, continued to maintain entail in the nineteenth century. It is tempting therefore to compare the *fideicommissum* with the strict family settlement. Conspicuously the *fideicommissum* was a more rigorous device. Like other Continental entails it was a perpetual entail, to be altered only by appeal to the crown or the courts. It was therefore a more certain preserver of landed estates. Nevertheless it was less popular than the strict family settlement. The *fideicommissum* covered about 5 percent of the land of Prussia in the 1850s. In a Junker province like Pomerania it covered about 15 percent.[34] The comparable figure for England, as we have seen, is 50 percent. These figures are all rough. Moreover they may not be strictly comparable. Any landowner in England could create an entail. A Prussian landowner required the sanction of the state. It is likely, nevertheless, that the figures point to a real difference in the popularity of entail in two countries where it remained available.

The Russian story is singular. Peter I had worried about land fragmentation and had legislated for impartibility, at least upon death. Landowners had objected and they had prevailed. Later tsars licensed a few entails for particular landowners. In 1845 a statute allowed entails for a limited class of landowners. Little Russian land was ever in entail—in 1914 far under one percent.[35] Russian landowners freely divided their estates in fee among their children male and female. The Russian novel provides examples of this. Thus in *Anna Karenina* Vronsky shared the family estate with his elder brother, and the dowry of the Princess Oblonsky comprised a country estate and a piece of forest. Consequently, as Russian historians point out, Russian estates tended to wander and to disintegrate.[36]

Two features stand out in the foregoing accounts and require discussion. The first is the nonemergence—practically speaking—of entail in Russia. Richard Pipes has recently argued that Russian landowners were averse to entail because their younger sons, if stripped of family property, had no source of income: "they were worse off than a peasant expelled from the commune."[37] There is no doubt that Russia lacked the rich commercial and professional life that often provided for the sons of the English landed elite. Even the Russian Orthodox Church, unlike the Church of England, failed to supply respectable employment for younger sons.[38] On the other hand, Russian sons found employment in the army and the bureaucracy, and for all we know these occupations may have compensated for a backward commercial life. Even if they did not, there is cause to be skeptical of Pipes's argument. After all, entail emerged in feudal Europe, where commerce was scarcely more flourishing than in nineteenth-century Russia. It would therefore seem that Russia's idiosyncrasy must be explained in other ways.

Not in the short supply of jobs for younger sons but in the political role of the Russian landed elite. As Professor Blum makes clear, the Russian was essentially a service nobility, and its real title to social eminence came from state service rather than land. Unlike the English landed elite, the Russian did not define itself in opposition to central authority. On the contrary, it acquiesced in that authority and was always completely dependent on it. It had thus early learned to be casual about its estates and their continuity, finding replenishment either through free gift or through cheap purchase from the land-wealthy state.[39] It found little reason for the self-discipline that the English landed elite, much less sustained by the central authority, had early found necessary.

The second feature requiring discussion is the decline of entail in the Continental countries where it had earlier flourished. In France, and then in Spain, entail was abolished by law. In Prussia, where it remained legal, it was little used. Prussian landowners in the nineteenth century held apparently that entails cost more than they were worth. While they guaranteed estate succession, they came ever more often to hinder the reasonable land transactions that agricultural and industrial improvement demanded. Significantly, Spanish landowners cheerfully accepted the abolition of the *mayorazgo* recognizing "that its effect would be to increase the value of their estates which would enter the ordinary commercial market";[40] and French landowners proved cool when Charles X attempted in 1826 to revive prerevolutionary entails.[41] Holding estates in fee involves risk for aristocracy—that was the raison d'être of entail—but safety from risk, it seems, could be bought too dear. Perhaps this indicates the "embourgeoisement" of the aristocracy. On the other hand, perhaps it indicates aristocratic self-confidence, a trust that spirit and habit would suffice to preserve estates.

Agricultural and industrial development clearly faced English landowners quite as much as Continental ones, but because English entail differed from Continental varieties in not being perpetual, it proved adaptable to the demands put upon it. The regular necessity for each father and son to renegotiate the family settlement led to the appearance of management provisions in settlements. As particular provisions became common, Parliament proceeded to make them universal by statute. By this means and others, English landowners managed, as the *Economist* put it, "to engraft rational progress on quasi-feudal tenures."[42] Accordingly, the strict family settlement proved the only useful legal device for preserving aristocratic estates in the nineteenth century.

This brings us to the habits of residence among the elites. It needs to be said at the start that habits of residence are not the same in all sections of an elite.[43] Wealthy families may have different habits from the less wealthy. Historians have often neglected this distinction, and have spoken as if the members of an elite all lived alike. Poorer landowners in all elites moved mainly in the small world of rural neighborhood, bound to the soil almost as much as their tenants or their peasants. Only with the coming of the railways did the habits of such landowners begin to change.

Having said this, we may venture less incautiously on a brief account of varying residential habits. Lewis Namier has said that English landowners were "amphibious."[44] By this he meant that they spent several months of the year in London—the so-called season—for a mixture of social and political reasons. He meant further that they brought to their rural existence an urban sophistication. All this is true: the English elite did live happily in two worlds, more successfully amphibious than any other landed elite. Nevertheless English landowners were at heart land animals. They spent the greater part of the year in the countryside. It was there that they built their principal houses; there that they kept their libraries and art collections; there that they laid out their gardens and parks, those visible symbols of the secret life of their imagination; and there that they indulged their obsession with killing game.

No other landed elite, with the exception of the Prussian, was as much resident upon its estates. The great Spanish landowners did not live in the countryside at all—"they would have found English countryhouse life inconceivable."[45] The French landed elite, who—at the upper levels at least—had been absentees in the eighteenth century, took to a sort of *vie de château* in the nineteenth century. How deeply rooted this was is doubtful. Nassau Senior, a close friend of Tocqueville and a visitor to his French country house, sensed there a sort of isolation, a lack of what the novelist Jane Austen called "neighborhood"—that is, an intimate community of neighboring landed families who frequently dined and danced and hunted together, the sort of community that lengthy residence would nurture. "Madame Anisson," Senior reported, "who has lived in English countryhouses in what are called good social neighborhoods, wondered at our liking such a life."[46]

Perhaps no other landed elite was so thoroughly detached from local roots as was the Russian. Its great owners rarely visited their estates, and its middling ones visited theirs only in the summer.[47] In Tolstoy's *Anna Karenina*, the families of the Levins and the Shterbatskys are described as "old noble Moscow families." How odd it would seem to call great English families like the Cavendishes and the Greys "old

London families"! This detachment from the land is made explicit by
one of the principal characters in the novel, Konstantin Levin. Levin's
aim in life is to set himself up as a resident country gentleman in the
English style. He is looked upon as an oddity, a misfit, even by himself. "He (he knew very well how he must appear to others) was a
country gentleman, occupied in breeding cattle, shooting game, and
building barns; in other words, a fellow of no ability, who had not
turned out well, and who was doing just what, according to the ideas
of the world, is done by people fit for nothing else."

Finally, there is the matter of estate management. In the present
state of research, it is difficult, if not impossible, to say very much
about this subject for any elite but the English. In what ways landowners contributed to the making of estate policy, what sort of men
they employed as agents, the machinery of estate management—much
is known about these things in England.[48] In the absence of such
information for the Continental elites, the most that can be done here
is to suggest some large differences in the sort of estate business that
the several elites dealt in.

In agricultural business, a crucial difference lay in the persistence on
the Continent of a large mass of small and backward farms, if not
owned then cultivated by peasants or serfs. The English landed elite
had early gone far in removing these inefficient cultivators and had put
in their place a substantial, businesslike tenantry and a landless proletariat working for wages. This meant that English landowners from
the eighteenth century onwards were disposed to promote productive
techniques and estate improvements. The Prussian landed elite attained
this disposition, but only during the first half of the nineteenth century in the course of emancipating its peasants. Prussian emancipation
benefited the landed elite much more than the peasants. Enriched by
two million acres of agricultural land previously owned by the peasants, Prussian landowners became rural entrepreneurs cultivating their
estates directly, aided only by a rural proletariat recruited from the
ranks of the peasantry.[49] Neither the Russian nor the French nor the
Spanish landed elites, however, ever managed to free themselves of the
peasant problem. The Russian emancipation of 1861 brought neither
land nor the spirit of enterprise to Russian landowners. In France and
Spain, peasant farming remained a major force in the countryside,
although during the second half of the nineteenth century it became
itself subject to currents of technological change.[50]

In the nonagricultural business of landed elites, probably the English went furthest in undertaking a wide variety of enterprise. If there were minerals under the land or a town site to develop, the English landowner rented his land to a mining operator or to a house builder. Sometimes, as did great owners like the Lambtons or the Wards, he mined his own coal and built forges and laid out canals and railways.[51] Continental landed elites, to be sure, were familiar with nonagricultural business. The French had known it under Louis XVI and knew it to a larger extent in the nineteenth century. They could then boast of, among others, a Comte Benoit d'Azy: agricultural improver, organizer of banks and railways, and leading ironmaster.[52] The Prussians had their Silesian coal-mining and iron-making families. Bismarck built lumber mills on his Varzin estate to exploit his extensive woodlands, and Bethmann Hollweg did very well out of brick making, no doubt to supply the needs of Berlin's remarkable growth.[53] Some of the great Russian landowners refined sugar, or made coarse woolen cloth in estate factories, or set up mining and metallurgical enterprises.[54] However, if it were possible to calculate the extent of nonagricultural business, it is likely that the English landed elite would be found outrunning Continental elites in raising (or helping to raise) such important crops as coal or urban houses. After all, the Industrial Revolution was an English invention, and English landowners readily lent themselves to its promotion. It was no accident that great English landowners like the Leveson Gowers and the Fitzwilliams took a leading part in the economic development of such nurseries of the Industrial Revolution as southeast Lancashire and the West Riding of Yorkshire. English profits were large and tempting; English aristocratic aversions to trade were weaker than the Continental; and English land law put fewer obstacles in the way of landowners' developing subsoil wealth than did Continental land law.[55]

II

"The true aristocratic theory of civil government," according to Matthew Arnold, gives primacy to local government: "with the local government in their hands . . . [landowners] do not wish to see the state overshadowing them and ordering them about."[56] In other words, for Arnold the key to landed power was to be found in the localities. Nineteenth-century landed elites seem to confirm this. Those elites that were strong nationally—the English, Prussian, and to a lesser extent the Spanish—in one way or another controlled their localities. Those elites that were not strong nationally—the French and the Russian—did not control their localities.

The English landed elite ruled the countryside through the justice of the peace, an unpaid oligarch who was usually a landowner. Rule by justices persisted deep into the nineteenth century—until the Local Government Act of 1888 installed in place of the appointed justices elected county councils. Although in some counties before 1888 there was a decline in the number of justices who were landowners, by and large landowners remained predominant.[57] Even after 1888 landowners were powerful in local government; up to the end of the century many of them were elected to the county councils.

The Prussian landed elite ruled the countryside through the bureaucratic *Landrat*, who was at once an official of the central government and the representative of the landowners. Prussia also had a locally elected assembly, the *Kreistag*, which was likewise dominated by the landed elite—at least until 1872.[58] The *Kreistag*, however, possessed small power compared to the *Landräte*, who remained the dominant force in local government. In spite of the fact that the office of *Landrat* became increasingly professionalized, "as late as 1914 well over half the *Landräte* in the eastern provinces were noblemen." In a prime Junker province like Pomerania the proportion in 1890 was about 90 percent.[59]

The Spanish landed elite ruled the countryside through *caciquismo*, a kind of bossism, as Professor Herr describes it in his paper. The *cacique* stood outside the official hierarchies: a local boss, a manipulator of votes, a dispenser of patronage. Unlike the Prussian *Landrat* or the English justice of the peace, his chief function was to circumvent the central government. This secret network of influence and power frustrated both bureaucratic and party agents in the localities and undermined the judiciary. Precisely what the relations between the landed elite and *caciquismo* were is not clear, but that the landed elite managed to get its way is clear enough.

The French and Russian landed elites, on the other hand, were weak locally. The *conseils généraux*, French equivalents of the Prussian *Kreistag* and the English county council, were not dominated by landowners. In 1840 only 17 percent of the councils were noblemen, and in 1870 only 27.6 percent.[60] The increase was probably due as much to the inflation of dubious titles as to the growth of landed influence. In any case, the number of nobles was not impressive. Even had it been, it would not have meant much. As Dr Zeldin points out, the councils "were never able to obtain very extensive power and the state-appointed prefect was . . . the more or less omnipotent authority at the local level." After 1830, moreover, the prefect was rarely a noble landowner, and the policy he administered was likely to favor the peasantry. In the mid-1850s Nassau Senior spelled out in detail the prefect's powers. "The Prefet appoints the Maires; the Prefet appoints in every canton a Commissaire de Police, . . . the Gardes champetres, who are the local police, are put under his control; the Rector, who was a sort of local Minister of Education in every department, is suppressed; his powers are transferred to the Prefet; the Prefet appoints, promotes and dismisses all the masters of the ecoles primaries. The Prefet can destroy the prosperity of every commune that displeases him . . . [he] can dissolve the Conseil general of his department, and although he cannot actually name their successors, he does so virtually."[61]

In Russia the central bureaucracy was always in control of the localities, and it controlled them not in the interest of landowners or merchants or of anyone else but in the interest of the state: "the [Russian] State," according to Professor Gerschenkron, "was not the State of this or that class. It was the State's State."[62] On occasion in the nineteenth century, the central bureaucracy encouraged landowners to run their local affairs, but it did not do so consistently nor for long. Significantly the emancipation of the serfs, that huge scheme of social engineering in the Russian countryside, was not the work of the landowners, who largely opposed it, but the work of the imperial bureaucracy.

The Prussian and English elites, strong in the localities, most clearly held on to the national power. How they used that power is worth pondering. The English landed elite governed the nation in a liberal and open spirit, the Prussian in an illiberal and closed one. In his book *Social Origins of Dictatorship and Democracy*, Barrington Moore dwells on these differences. As he sees it, the English landed elite was something of a freak—having broken away from the standard type. This type, represented by the Prussians, arose from certain social elements: a bureaucratic monarchy, an oppressed peasantry, a blood and soil ideology, and a timid middle class. The last, Barrington Moore sees as the key element. In England the middle class was strong, long rooted in a tradition of freedom, capable of imposing its outlook on the rest of society. Accordingly, the English landed elite, Barrington Moore seems to suggest, was but a coroneted version of the English middle class, prizing freedom because it had no choice in the matter.[63]

There is some truth in this, but it is not the whole truth. Love of liberty inhered in the collective mentality of the English landed elite itself. Rather than being forced by a new class to be libertarian, the English landed elite was fundamentally disposed to be so. Historically it had defined itself against the crown, against the principles of autocracy, against the maintenance of large standing armies. At bottom, this was what that landlords' assembly otherwise known as Parliament stood for. Parliament, in turn, helped school the nation in liberal practices and a liberal spirit. Thus it may be said that the influence of the landed elite moved downwards in society. Professor Thompson vividly demonstrates in his paper how the landed elite in some ways stamped the middle class—or a part of it—with its own "cast of ideas," to use a phrase of Matthew Arnold's.

Two examples may help to illustrate this libertarian disposition. Between 1815 and 1822 the English government took to a repressive Toryism and, according to Barrington Moore, might well have turned Junker. At that very time, however, a large part of the English governing class—the Whiggish part—was fiercely conducting county meetings throughout the English countryside. Much about these meetings was hardly Junkerlike. Often attended by hundreds, sometimes thousands, of persons of all social classes, these large public assemblies freely and openly discussed the leading issues of the day, concluding with a series of resolutions drawn up in the form of parliamentary petitions. To an Austrian nobleman who was present at a Kentish county meeting in 1822 this display of free discussion under the auspices of a disputatious aristocracy was an astonishing sight—as he put it, an extraordinary mixture of democracy and aristocracy nowhere else to be found in Europe.[64]

English landowners also displayed their liberal principles in supporting the politics of Italian unification. For them Garibaldi was a hero. In his famous visit to London in 1864, he was driven through tumultuous London crowds in the carriage of the duke of Sutherland—whose duchess later took him to Eton to receive the cheers of aristocratic schoolboys.[65] For Prussian landowners, the hero's mantle fell not on Garibaldi but on Francis II, king of Naples, whom Garibaldi had driven into exile.[66] To this inglorious if unfortunate monarch, Prussian noblemen presented a silver shield as a token of their admiration. On it the king was depicted "slaying numerous revolutionary demons . . . crowned with the brightest crown of martyrdom" and was lauded as "the last and the noblest of the great principle of legitimacy."[67]

This libertarian disposition led the English landed elite to play a creative part in the shaping of free institutions in the nineteenth century—a fact that is often overlooked. After all, governments led by the landed elite opened up both central and local government to the scrutiny of public opinion. They also put an end to a House of Commons dominated by aristocratic factions and replaced it with a House of Commons dominated by the party system, that political invention central to an age of free discussion. The party system was a vehicle of self-criticism, a political game with its own imperatives, compelling enough to lead the disputatious landed elite willy-nilly to unforeseen places and not wholly intended results. In time the age of discussion grew uncongenial to the landed elite. Not only did the argument persist in going against it but the discussion itself became too much of a hurly-burly—too technical, too time-consuming, often too expensive. Nonetheless, the landed elite, as Professor Thompson has pointed out, did not overturn the institutions of free public discussion, but simply retired from the scene. It submitted in the end to the force of the argument. As Tocqueville once noted, this was the most liberal aristocracy in the history of the world.[68]

On the other hand, Prussian landowners were never lovers of public disputation or of parliaments. As Professor Stern's paper makes clear, what they loved best next to their estates was an army and all that went with it—splendid uniforms, military pomp, and chivalric codes of honor. From this soil came the distinctive Junker mentality, which found little to inhibit it in a society where public discussion was subdued if not outlawed.[69] Accordingly, a conservative agrarianism was more alive at the end of the nineteenth century in Prussia than anything approaching it had ever been in England.[70] Fifty years after the English landed elite submitted to the repeal of agricultural protection, the Prussian successfully fought for its retention with a fierceness and ingenuity that made earlier English efforts seem supine.[71] The Prussians brooked no opposition. It never occurred to them to accept any other argument but their own.

This essay may well end with a brief appeal to the new generation of social historians, which has shown a fondness for subjects like collective mentality, demography, and the family. So far, these historians have looked downwards in society, believing that the densely populated depths have been neglected. No one would argue with this. It is worthwhile, however, to bring to their attention the riches that may be found should they turn their gaze upwards to study landed elites. Here their new interests could be amply indulged. What better place

to study family structure and dynamics? Landed elites are made up of
families who, being prone to self-commemoration, leave behind them
great quantities of revealing documentation. Their vanity well serves
the historian's uses, and their records should be explored more fully.

NOTES

1. A. Goodwin, ed., *The European Nobility in the Eighteenth Century: Studies
of the Nobilities of the Major European States in the Pre-Reform Era* (London,
1953).
2. Barrington Moore, Jr., *Social Origins of Dictatorship and Democracy in the
Making of the Modern World* (Boston, 1966).
3. M. Bloch, "Pour une histoire comparée des sociétés européennes," *Revue
de synthèse historique* 46 (1928), reprinted and translated in F. C. Lane and J. C.
Riemersma, eds., *Enterprise and Secular Change: Readings in Economic History*
(Homewood, Illinois, 1953), p. 507. It is useful to read in conjunction with Bloch's
essay, W. H. Sewell, Jr., "Marc Bloch and the Logic of Comparative History,"
History and Theory 6 (1967): 208–18.
4. For French statistics, see G. W. Grantham, "Scale and Organization in
French Farming, 1840–1880," in W. N. Parker and E. L. Jones, *European Peasants
and Their Market: Essays in Agrarian Economic History* (Princeton, 1975). For
Prussian statistics (for the years 1882, 1895, and 1907), see K. Grünberg, "Agrarverfassung," *Grundriss der Sozialökonomik* 7 (1922): 131–67. I am indebted for the
latter reference to Professor James Sheehan of Northwestern University.
5. British Parliamentary Papers (hereafter cited as B.P.P.), 1874, LXXII, *Return
of Owners of Land, 1872–3.* The raw data of the parliamentary return were ab-
stracted and organized by John Bateman in *The Great Landowners of Great
Britain and Ireland.* In the final edition of this work, published in 1883, Bateman
listed all landowners owning 2000 acres and more and indicated their total holdings county by county. This was a valuable service.
6. F. M. L. Thompson, *English Landed Society in the Nineteenth Century*
(London, 1963), pp. 28–29, 31, 112–13.
7. Bateman, *Great Landowners*, p. 515. The figures for smaller private owners
and for public bodies refer to England and Wales and are thus not strictly comparable to the figures for the large owners, which refer to England alone. To
have made them so would have involved a great deal of work to little purpose:
the order of magnitude is accurate enough.
8. *Statistique agricole de la France: Résultats généraux de l'enquête décennale
de 1882* (Nancy, 1887), pp. 280–81.
9. Lord Montagu of Beaulieu, *More Equal than Others: The Changing Fortunes
of the British and European Aristocracies* (London, 1970), p. 57; B.P.P., 1890–1,
LXXXIII, *Reports from H.M.'s Representatives Abroad on the Position of Peasant Proprietors*, p. 47.
10. P. Goubert, "Le paysan et la terre: Seigneurie, tenure, exploitation," in
F. Braudel and E. Labrousse, eds., *Histoire économique et sociale de la France*
(Paris, 1970), 2:119–59.
11. Quoted in G. G. Richardson, *The Corn and Cattle Producing Districts of
France* (London, 1878), p. 32.
12. R. Forster, "The Survival of the Nobility during the French Revolution,"
Past & Present, July 1967, pp. 71–87. I should add that Forster estimates that the

Toulouse nobleman suffered heavier losses in his nonagricultural income, which would have increased his vulnerability as a landowner.

13. Presumably following Labrousse, Forster estimates that the average noble holding in eighteenth-century France was 370 acres.

14. In an 1842 letter to his sister; see R. Disraeli, ed., *Lord Beaconsfield's Correspondence with His Sister 1823–52* (London, 1886), p. 182. Disraeli also declared that "there are only one hundred men [landowners, presumably] who have £10,000 per annum." Was this an invention of Disraeli's fertile imagination?

15. This statistical information is taken from the following reports: B.P.P., 1870, LXVII, *Reports from H.M.'s Representatives respecting the Tenure of Land in the Several Countries of Europe*, p. 355; B.P.P., 1890–1, LXXXIII, *Reports . . . on the Position of Peasant Proprietors*, p. 54. Both of these reports are based on the Prussian statistics of the 1850s which, it would seem, provide information on the number of estates and landowners as distinct from the number of farms. Later German statistics (for 1882, 1895, and 1907), it would seem, confine themselves to farms.

16. See K. Grünberg, "Agrarverfassung," *Grundriss der Sozialökonomik*, p. 138.

17. B.P.P., 1870, LXVII, *Reports . . . respecting the Tenure of Land*, p. 319, for a useful table on the *Rittergüter*.

18. The first statement comes from T. S. Hamerow, *Restoration, Revolution, Reaction: Economics and Politics in Germany, 1815–1871* (Princeton, 1958), p. 226; the second statement comes from W. Abel, *Agrarkrisen und Agrarkonjunctur: Eine Geschichte der Land-und Ernährungswirtschaft Mitteleuropas seit dem hohen Mittelalter* (Hamburg and Berlin, 1966), pp. 253–56. I am indebted to Professor Jerome Blum for this latter reference.

19. There is a suggestion of this point in K. E. Born, "Structural Changes in German Social and Economic Development at the end of the Nineteenth Century," in J. J. Sheehan, ed., *Imperial Germany* (New York, 1976), p. 24.

20. Of the 15,000 large estates in Prussia in the 1850s, only about 4,000 were *Rittergüter* (B.P.P., 1870, LXVII, *Reports . . . respecting the Tenure of Land*, p. 355). This being the case, to say (as is often said) that only 57 percent of the *Rittergüter* in the 1850s were in noble hands may also exaggerate the displacement of traditional authority. The source of this exaggeration is the classic article by Hans Rosenberg, "Die 'Demokratisierung' der Rittergütbesitzer Klasse," in W. Berges and C. Hinrichs, eds., *Zur Geschichte und Problematik der Demokratie: Festgabe für Hans Herzfeld* (Berlin, 1958).

21. B.P.P., 1871, LXVII, *Reports . . . respecting the Tenure of Land*, p. 19.

22. E. E. Malefakis, *Agrarian Reform and Peasant Revolution in Spain: Origins of the Civil War* (New Haven and London, 1970), pp. 420–21.

23. J. Blum, *Lord and Peasant in Russia: From the Ninth to the Nineteenth Century* (Princeton, 1962), p. 370.

24. M. G. Mulhall, *The Dictionary of Statistics*, 4th ed. (London, 1899), p. 340.

25. For an account of strict family settlement in practice, see E. Spring, "The Settlement of Land in Nineteenth-Century England," *American Journal of Legal History* 8, no. 3 (July 1964), pp. 209–24.

26. Thompson, *English Landed Society*, p. 68.

27. See the helpful "Glossary, Chart, Maps and Bibliography" on French inheritance laws presented by R. Giesey, E. Richards, and R. Wheaton to the Society for French Historical Studies, 9–10 April 1976. Of course, division of property does not necessarily mean the physical division of landed estates. There might be sufficient nonlanded property to allow the land to remain intact; or mortgages might be raised on the land to pay the portions of younger children.

28. See R. Forster, *The Nobility of Toulouse in the Eighteenth Century* (Baltimore, 1960), chapter 6; and *The House of Saulx-Tavanes: Versailles and Burgundy, 1700–1830* (Baltimore, 1971).

29. T. Zeldin, *France 1848–1945* (Oxford, 1973), p. 144.

30. J. Tulard, "Problèmes sociaux de la France impériale," *Revue d'histoire moderne et contemporaine*, July–Sept. 1970, pp. 639–63. I am indebted to Professor Frederick Gillen of the State University of New York for this reference and for information on the *majorat*.

31. E. Cecil, *Primogeniture: A Short History of Its Development in Various Countries and Its Practical Effects* (London, 1895), p. 109.

32. J. Brissaud, *A History of French Private Law* (Boston, 1912), p. 733.

33. Malefakis, *Agrarian Reform*, p. 68.

34. B.P.P., 1870, LXVII, *Reports . . . respecting the Tenure of Land*, p. 290. In the enlarged post-1870 Prussia, the area covered by the *fideicommissum* was about the same (see B.P.P., 1896, LXXXIV, *General and Detailed Reports . . . on the Systems of Registration of Title*, p. 40).

35. A. M. Anfimov, *Krupnoe pomeshchich'e khoziaistvo evropeiskoi Rossii* (Moscow, 1969), pp. 43–46. I am indebted to Professor Blum for this reference.

36. See, among others, M. Raeff, *Origins of the Russian Intelligentsia. The Eighteenth Century Nobility* (New York, 1966), chap. 3.

37. R. Pipes, *Russia under the Old Regime* (London, 1974), p. 176.

38. On the Russian Orthodox church, see Pipes, pp. 243–44. On the Prussian Lutheran church and younger sons, see remarks of the crown princess of Prussia (who was English) in R. Fulford, ed., *Your Dear Letter* (New York, 1971), p. 86; and on the Catholic church in France and younger sons, see M. C. M. Simpson, ed., *Correspondence and Conversations of Alexis de Tocqueville with Nassau William Senior*, 2 vols. (London, 1872), 1:163.

39. It is sometimes also suggested that Russian land banks propped up landed finances to the extent of tolerating defaulters, but in the absence of detailed studies of Russian (and other) land banks, one hesitates to accept such an odd notion about banks.

40. J. Nadal, "Spain 1830–1914," in C. Cipolla, ed., *The Fontana Economic History of Europe: The Emergence of Industrial Societies* (London, 1973), p. 555.

41. I am indebted to Professor Frederick Gillen for this information.

42. *The Economist* (London), Jan. 5, 1856.

43. Raymond Carr puts this point succinctly: "There were differing levels of absenteeism at differing levels of the noble's world." R. Carr, *Spain, 1808–1939* (Oxford, 1966), p. 41.

44. Lewis Namier, *England in the Age of the American Revolution* (London, 1931), p. 16.

45. Carr, *Spain*, p. 42.

46. Simpson, *Correspondence . . . of de Tocqueville with William Nassau Senior*, 1:169. Tocqueville himself noticed the difference (Simpson, 1:114–15).

47. T. Emmons, *The Russian Landed Gentry and the Peasant Emancipation of 1861* (London, 1968), chap. 1.

48. See D. Spring, *The English Landed Estate in the Nineteenth Century: Its Administration* (Baltimore, 1963).

49. For a recent account of Prussian emancipation and agricultural development, see R. A. Dickler, "Organization and Change in Productivity in Eastern Prussia," in Parker and Jones, *European Peasants and Their Markets*.

50. For a recent account of French peasant farming, see G. W. Grantham, "Scale and Organization in French Farming, 1840–1880," in Parker and Jones, *European Peasants and Their Markets*.

51. For an account of such enterprise, see D. Spring, "English Landowners and Nineteenth-Century Industrialism," in J. T. Ward and R. G. Wilson, eds., *Land and Industry: The Landed Estate and the Industrial Revolution* (Newton Abbot, 1971).

52. P. Goubert, *Ancien Regime: French Society 1600–1750* (New York, 1974), p. 169; R. R. Locke, *French Legitimists and the Politics of Moral Order in the Early Third Republic* (Princeton, 1974), pp. 106–11.

53. H. Holborn, *A History of Modern Germany 1880–1945* (New York, 1969),

p. 126; G. W. Curtis, ed., *The Correspondence of John L. Motley*, 3 vols. (New York, 1900), 3:275; K. H. Jarausch, *The Enigmatic Chancellor: Bethmann Hollweg and the Hubris of Imperial Germany* (New Haven, 1973), p. 14. Forestry was also a lucrative source of income and together with brickmaking brought in more than farming on the Bethmann Hollweg estate.

54. W. L. Blackwell, *The Beginnings of Russian Industrialisation* (Princeton, 1968), pp. 198–204.

55. For Continental land law, see B.P.P., 1887, LXXXI, *Reports by H.M.'s Representatives Abroad on Mining Rents and Royalties*, pp. 8–9; also B.P.P., 1893–4, XLI, *Fourth Report of the Royal Commission on Mining Royalties*, pp. 285–86. For urban development on the Continent, see B.P.P., 1896, LXXXIV, *General and Detailed Reports . . . on the System of Registration of Title*, p. 12; also B.P.P., 1884, LXXXIII, *Reports of H.M.'s Representatives Abroad upon the System of Tenure of Dwelling Houses*, p. 13. Some English landowners like the Howards and the Russells owned valuable market rights in cities like Sheffield and London, but these too did not exist on the Continent (see B.P.P., 1890–1, XLI, *Royal Commission on Market Rights and Tolls*, pp. 14–15).

56. Matthew Arnold, *Democratic Education*, ed. R. H. Super (Ann Arbor, 1962), pp. 5, 304.

57. I base this statement on the incomplete doctoral dissertation of Robert Shorthouse, who is examining closely the justices in five English counties, 1790–1889.

58. R. M. Berdahl, "Conservative Politics and Aristocratic Landholders in Bismarckian Germany," *Journal of Modern History*, March 1972, pp. 1–21.

59. L. W. Muncy, "The Prussian Landräte in the Last Years of the Monarchy: A Case Study of Pomerania and the Rhineland in 1890–1918," *Central European History*, December 1973, pp. 299–338.

60. A. J. Tudesq, "Les survivances de l'ancien régime: La noblesse dans la société française de la première moitié du XIXe siècle," in D. Roche and C. E. Labrousse, *Orders et classes: Colloque d'histoire sociale* (St. Cloud, 1967), pp. 203–4.

61. Simpson, *Correspondence . . . of de Tocqueville with William Nassau Senior*, 2: 114–15.

62. A. Gerschenkron, *Europe in the Russian Mirror: Four Lectures in Economic History* (Cambridge, 1970), p. 79.

63. See especially Moore, *Social Origins*, pp. 418–25. Sometimes Moore suggests that the bourgeoisie did not always have its own way, but this is not the dominant impression left by his book. See also the most searching of the reviews of Moore's book by R. Dore, "Making Sense of History," *Archives européennes de sociologie* 10 (1969): 295–305.

64. A. de Stael-Holstein, *Letters on England* (London, 1825), pp. 120–21, 184, 196–97.

65. G. M. Trevelyan, *Garibaldi and the Making of Italy* (London, 1911), pp. 289–90.

66. For a sympathetic portrait of Francis II, see H. Acton, *The Last Bourbons of Naples* (New York, 1961).

67. *Saturday Review* (London), October 14, 1865.

68. A. de Tocqueville, *Democracy in America*, trans. H. Reeve, 2 vols. (New York, 1900), 2:244.

69. Karl Mannheim has an interesting discussion on this point in *Essays on Sociology and Social Psychology*, ed. P. Kekskemeti (New York, 1953), chap. 2. For the comparatively xenophobic atmosphere of Junker society, see L. Cecil, "Jew and Junker in Imperial Berlin," *Yearbook* of the Leo Baeck Institute, 1975.

70. See K. D. Barkin, *Controversy over German Industrialization 1890–1902* (Chicago, 1970).

71. See A. Gerschenkron, *Bread and Democracy in Germany* (Berkeley, 1943), pp. 26–27.

F. M. L. THOMPSON

2 | Britain

That splendid English game of cricket, which foreigners and females of every nationality find so unfailingly tedious, was first nurtured from local obscurity into national addiction by the exploits and patronage of the nobility and gentry. The lead was taken in the first half of the nineteenth century by the Reverend Lord Frederick Beauclerk, vicar of Redbourne in Hertfordshire, whose outstanding skill as a batsman gave him whatever social authority he may have lacked as the fourth son of the fifth duke of St Albans.[1] It was during his rule that the Gentlemen v. Players match became established as one of the leading events of the season. Tried experimentally in 1806, it was revived in 1819 and was thereafter played annually at Lord's until 1962, apart from the years of war. It was a match between the leisured, amateur, unpaid, gentry on one side, and the professional, paid, working cricketers on the other; except that in order to keep the fixture going at all in its last dozen years it became necessary to permit the gentry to include some players in their team. Then by 1962 there were no longer any gentry left whose skills were a match for those of the players, and this particular English tradition disappeared. It was a tradition rooted in the deference society of aristocratic, landowning, England. What is more, it was a tradition whose history mirrored not merely the relations between old and new elements in British society but also the course traveled by the landed elite in its passage from supremacy to retreat into the position of cultivated and knowledgeable spectators. The ruling elite, confronted from the late eighteenth century by the new social and economic forces generated by population growth, urbanization, and industrialization, at first kept the game of power and influence in its own hands, simply allowing its ranks to expand a little by the carefully controlled admission of a few new men who could pay the proper entry fee. Then the techniques of accommodation were extended by permitting the new men to join in the game, provided they did not win too often, and provided their acceptability was established by adequate sieving and screening. Nevertheless, in the end the circumstances and functions of government, politics, social life, and income getting changed so profoundly that there were no longer enough landed gentlemen with sufficient leisure or skill to keep up the tone, and the field of power and influence was left to the active, working, professional players. Some of these were members of old landed families, obliged to abandon their amateur status. Some were traditional new men, from banking, commerce, industry, and the professions; others were newer new men, from the trade unions, the large corporations, and the mass media. Taken together they made up a new ruling elite, a new Establishment; the old landed elite had retired to the wings, almost literally to the royal enclosure at Ascot, thence to observe the great world go by.

When, why, and how all this came to pass are questions which embrace the whole of British history since the Industrial Revolution, and it would be idle to pretend that the application of techniques of miniaturization and encapsulation to historiography is so advanced that the answers can be presented in a couple of equations and a footnote. In this chapter attention will be concentrated instead on just one feature, the aristocratic embrace, that process and technique which served the aristocracy so well in maintaining a preponderance for the landed elite right through to 1914. The process involved, in a graphic Trollopian phrase, the established aristocracy "gobbling up" the new men of no family and little fortune as they came knocking at the doors of the great world of high society and high politics, attracting, luring, or enslaving them with the seductive charms, favors, and graces that aristocratic people and aristocratic living could provide. Ramsay MacDonald is generally held to have been one of the last, if not the last, leading radical and paper revolutionary to have been tamed by the aristocratic embrace and to have been flattered into docility and moderation by being lionized.[2] It may well be that the process continued to be effective in the 1920s, and indeed that it still is in the 1970s; but in the face of the weight of conventional wisdom, not to say the apparent weight of the evidence, it is sufficient for present purposes to contend for the continued dominance of the landed elite until the outbreak of the First World War.

No one would deny that in 1830 social and political power was firmly in the hands of the landed class, and that the actual positions of control and decision making were even more securely in the hands of a landed elite group. Similarly for the mid-Victorian period, the years of Trollope, few would now deny that the franchise changes of

1832 had not made very much difference, and that the syncopation of country-house politics and London society left control very much where it had always been, with top jobs and key positions occupied by the landed elite. By 1914, however, most historians have argued that the picture had changed, that the political elite had ceased to be a characteristically landed one, that the old landed aristocracy had slipped a long way towards merging into an upper class of varied origins, and that the ambience of political and social life had lost its flavor of aristocratic taste and breeding.[3] Many factors worked in these directions. The franchise extensions of 1867 and 1884, the secret ballot and the limitation of election expenses, the abolition of traditional constituencies in favor of single-member seats in 1885, all these tended to undermine the traditional constituency politics of influence and to increase the power of party machines and the openings for carpetbaggers. The decline in land values and in agricultural rents that affected many landed estates in the last quarter of the century meant that many landowners retrenched on the cost of politics, where formerly they might have been "inevitable" Parliament men. The increasing polarization of party politics from the 1870s, culminating in the great Whig secession of 1886, meant that members of landowning families tended to be concentrated on one side of the House. Finally, it is possible that more large fortunes were made after the 1880s than before—of the gold and diamonds variety as well as in more traditional banking, mining, shipowning, or brewing fashion—and that these millionaires, aided by the stream of less wealthy but socially ambitious company directors created by the trend to convert family firms into limited companies from the 1890s onwards, gave to society its reputation for growing hedonism and ostentation in the 1890s and 1900s, so often contrasted with the gravity and probity of high Victorian, and high aristocratic, London.[4]

These are powerful reasons for believing that somewhere between 1880 and the First World War the landed elite went into a decline, suffered a collapse, or at the very least went through a sea change transforming it by absorption into something different. Other considerations will, indeed, be introduced later which point in the same direction. At the moment, however, it is necessary to qualify the extent of any pre-1914 decline or collapse. If we look solely at the matter of the political elite, the change in the social composition of the House of Commons seems decisive and unsettling for land. Thus members of landed families provided at least three-quarters of the Commons in the 1840s, and still supplied two-thirds of the House in 1868. By 1886 the proportion had fallen to one-half, and indeed the

Parliament of 1880 has been greeted as the first in which the business-men and industrialists constituted a majority.[5] In the 1906 and 1910 Parliaments landed families, on comparable definitions, probably did not supply a great deal more than one-tenth of the Commons.[6] The figures are much affected by the results of particular elections, since the number of landowning M.P.'s declined much more steeply in the Liberal than in the Conservative party. The two elections of 1910 produced in all 1,531 candidates from all parties, of whom only 11 percent belonged to the landed interest (defined to consist of land-owners, country gentlemen, and farmers). If the farmers are excluded from this group, as being somewhat below the salt, then the Conserva-tives put 100 landed gentry into the field among their slate of 712 candidates, compared with only 44 landed Liberals in a total of 607 contestants.[7] By any reckoning there had been steep, even precipitous, decline since 1880. In the inner political elite, however, in membership of the cabinet, the landowning classes held their own much longer. It perhaps goes without saying that cabinets between the first and second Reform Bills were predominantly aristocratic in composition and strongly weighted with members of the House of Lords.[8] The very few men of no family who made the grade included only one, Disraeli, who reached the top of the greasy pole; in getting there he adopted the outward style and trimmings of a landowner even if he could never pretend to have shared the origins or upbringing of an aristo-crat. The rest of the new men who held cabinet office in this period were chiefly lawyers, and success in the law leading to occupation of the woolsack in any case nearly always led to social acclimatization, with country estates to match the peerages. After 1868 new men began to reach cabinet rank in appreciably greater numbers. Some were genuinely new men like Bright, Forster, Stansfeld, or Chamber-lain, who did not aspire to set themselves up as landed gentlemen. Others were less certainly new men like R. A. Cross, who was a younger son of a Lancashire squire and made an appearance in Burke's *Landed Gentry* in his own right with his seat at Eccles Rigg; H. A. Bruce, who amassed a large landed estate in south Wales, even if he did start life as a grammar school boy; and W. H. Smith, who put a considerable amount of the family bookstall fortune into land, even if he had been brought up a Methodist and had a highly successful business career.[9] Lord Randolph Churchill delighted in referring to Cross and Smith as "Marshall & Snelgrove," but after their fashion they were closer to the land than to drapery. Nevertheless, between 1868 and 1886 the cabinet continued to be dominated by men of the traditional type, and fully two-thirds of the 49 cabinet members were either from landowning families or from families closely linked with the aristocracy in the church, the services, and diplomacy.[10]

Between 1886 and 1916 the aristocratic element in cabinets dropped to one-half, and new men came flocking in. Few of these were on the Conservative side, where apart from the old hands like Cross, Smith, and Chamberlain perhaps only lesser figures like Ritchie and Akers-Douglas can be added to the list of new men until at the very end of the period Bonar Law joined the 1915 coalition. This was to be expected of a party that was run through the Hotel Cecil and that could readily recruit the services of country gentlemen like Chaplin, Hicks-Beach, and Walter Long should the supply of dukes, marquises, and their nephews prove insufficient. The case was different with the Liberal party after it had shed most of the Whig grandees, and by the 1900s it would seem that the Liberal party was in the hands of the middle class. The leaders were first Campbell-Bannerman, son of a very wealthy Scottish industrialist who had, however, taken the customary step of acquiring a country seat and estate to match; and after him Asquith, a barrister of humble origins.[11] Among the other leading figures Lloyd George, Haldane, Bryce, Morley, Birrell, and McKenna were all middle-class politicians, and they probably outranked as well as outnumbered the surviving Liberal aristocrats like Crewe, Ripon, and Carrington in the Lords, and Sir Edward Grey and Winston Churchill in the Commons.

Asquith, it may be argued, was the first of the modern prime ministers who did not spring from a landed family or an aristocratic background. But although he was definitely a more authentically middle-class figure than either Gladstone or Disraeli, or indeed than his fellow barrister George Canning with his typically aristocratic upbringing of Eton and Christ Church and entry into the House of Commons at the age of twenty-four, it would be rash to conclude that Asquith had no aristocratic streak. The streak was revealed by Margot. During his first marriage Asquith had been content to live in Hampstead leading the quiet and respectable life of an intellectual lawyer making his way in politics, giving no sign of wishing to mix in London society. The vivacious, impetuous Margot whisked him off to Cavendish Square and into the mainstream of the high society of the 1890s. The move was an enormous success, and the combination of his brilliance, Margot's wit and large circle of friends, and Tennant money made him widely known among the fashionable and the influential, and undoubtedly helped to bring him to the top. Asquith may never have taken to the country side of society life, disliking physical exercise—"I don't run much," he is said to have replied when urged to run to catch a train[12]—and being indifferent to hunting and shooting, but he enjoyed the more political and cultivated part of the London season as much as his wife did. This of course does not make a politician an aristocrat, though it does put him within reach of the aristocratic embrace. Asquith did not seek to turn political power into wealth and honor for himself, accepting an earldom only at the end of his career as an ex-prime minister's due, but he did seek aristocratic advancement and attachment through his family and for his family, and this was the next best thing to the time-honored process of founding a landed family. The Tennant family, well landed at Glen in Peeblesshire since 1852 out of the proceeds of the Glasgow chemical business, was not forgotten. Although his father-in-law died in 1906 before Asquith had the distribution of honors, he did not delay long before making his brother-in-law Lord Glenconner in 1911. More telling, perhaps, were the connections made by Asquith's children. In 1907, Raymond, his eldest and favorite son, married Katherine Horner, whose father Sir John was a considerable landowner in Somerset of old-established family and whose mother Frances was a leading society lady of the 1890s as well as being such a close friend of the Asquiths that she both received their confidences and lent them the Horner family seat of Mells Park for their honeymoon.[13] So this was an instance of the touching case of son marrying daughter of parents' best friends. It was rather different lower down the list. Asquith's second son married in 1910 Lady Cynthia, eldest daughter of the eleventh earl of Wemyss, an alliance with the ancient nobility all the more striking because before his succession to the earldom Wemyss had been Lord Elcho, son of the Adullamite and himself a Unionist—not a political acquaintance on Asquith's side of the game, but then Lady Elcho was one of the more prominent hostesses of the day. The third son, Arthur, followed the same pattern when he married Betty Manners in 1918. She was the daughter of the third Lord Manners, and her mother, whom Margot described as "my greatest friend," was also one of those clever and gracious ladies who had "the whole of London at her feet" in the 1890s.[14] Only the last son, Cyril, broke new ground by marrying in 1918 Anne Pollock, daughter of Sir Adrian Donald Wilde Pollock, barrister and City Chamberlain and cousin of the legal historian. Of Asquith's daughters, Violet followed an old route when she married her father's private secretary, Maurice Bonham-Carter; the surprise, if any, was that her father should have chosen a member of the landed gentry as his private secretary. Quite unsurprisingly Elizabeth, his daughter by his marriage with Margot, made a characteristically exotic match by walking off with a Roumanian prince, Antoine Bibesco.[15]

All this amounted to a tally of good matches so impressive that many a duchess or countess of impeccable pedigree would have been proud of it. That Asquith was also proud of it seems to say two things about the last Liberal prime minister. First, that Liberal politics did not seriously threaten aristocratic values, institutions, or possessions. The alternative explanation, that politics and family life were kept in separate compartments, is untenable in the light of the central role that politics played in defining the social circle of a family like the Asquiths, although it must be admitted that socially he probably saw a good deal more of Balfour, congenial though a political opponent, than he did of Lloyd George, a cabinet colleague and next-door neighbor.[16] Second, that the lure of high society, the attractions of its more cultivated and intellectually adventurous members, and the charms of the aristocratic embrace had once more done their work. There is no suggestion that the Asquiths set out on any tufthunting expeditions through their children, or in any way tried to arrange suitable marriages for them. The marriages, rather, grew naturally and spontaneously out of the social circle in which they were brought up, a circle enlarged but not altered by the childrens' contributions of smart and brilliant friends they made at Oxford. It is precisely the unforced, uncontrived, character of the alliances that shows how thoroughly and completely Asquith had been absorbed into the world of the upper-class elite. Later on, the position of the family, as well as the diversity of its talents, was confirmed by the career of the youngest son, Anthony, renowned as the only truly aristocratic film director of his generation.[17] It had been largely Margot's doing, though as suitor and as husband Asquith scarcely behaved like a reluctant victim. Margot herself had the entrée to society through beauty, wit, intelligence, wealth, and high spirits, but she was hardly of ancient lineage even though she had been brought up in the world of hunting and of country houses, and her father had been made a baronet. The society itself, however, was not a society of wealthy *nouveaux riches*, but one still organized and led by the established aristocracy, with active country centres in houses like Hatfield, Chatsworth, Dalmeny, and Bowood, and with the town houses that mattered managed by the likes of a duchess of Sutherland, a Lady Jersey, or a Lady Wemyss. So long as the tone continued to be set by members of the established aristocracy, and newcomers conformed to their habits and values, the society over which they presided remained an essentially landed elite. It seems that one must look further afield than Asquith for the first modern, nonlanded, prime minister; perhaps no further than Lloyd George, the ungentlemanly manner of whose arrival in power in 1916 was perfectly timed to coincide with the disintegration of the aristocratic order. The hour of the working politician had arrived as the player, Lloyd George, wrested the captaincy from the gentleman, Asquith.

The regime lasted so long less because of the flexibility of the social arrangements operated by the aristocracy than because of the unflagging quest for social acceptance and social advancement on the part of families coming up from below. At the same time it must be admitted that there was adaptability at the top. Partly this consisted of accepting newcomers into the ranks of landowning families, and partly of extending the circle of people who were admitted into high society. By the time of Victoria's accession the process of wealth gained in banking, trade, or industry being used to found a landed family that in due course became accepted in county society was already centuries old. There is not much evidence that it continued in the nineteenth century on an enlarged or expanding scale, merely that it continued. Its continuance was surprising only on economic grounds, since there were so many other investment opportunities available which were two or three times more profitable than landed estate. As *The Economist* argued in 1867, however, the motives for land purchase were primarily social. It instanced a Lancashire mill owner buying a country estate for the sake of the sport that could be offered to his sons and their new friends from Eton and Cambridge, and for the status of country gentleman for himself, with the prospect of a seat on the bench, "the sherrifalty, a squeeze of the hand from the Lord Lieutenant, the County balls for his wife and daughters, and perhaps an opening to the House of Commons."[18] A few years earlier the same paper had remarked disparagingly on the great capitalists who advertised in the newspapers their desire to lay out large sums of money in land, and on their employment of agents in several counties to make enquiries after eligible purchases, all to acquire status and "perhaps with an eye to the peerage." By 1870, still observing the same phenomenon, *The Economist* had changed its tune, observing that: "Social consideration is a great and legitimate object of desire, and so great is the effect of this visibility of wealth upon social consideration that it would pay a millionaire in England to sink half his fortune in buying 10,000 acres of land to return a shilling percent, and live upon the remainder, rather than to live upon the whole without land. He would be a greater person in the eyes of more people. The land is worth more to him to yield nothing than the Consols he sells to procure it—a state of affairs which makes competition with millionaires for such land nearly hopeless, and which will nevertheless remain permanent."[19]

It might be supposed that the drive to acquire status was in itself strong enough to sustain the status-conferring mechanisms of landed society, since those seeking the benefits of acceptance were most unlikely to wish to bite the only hand which could feed them, the hand of an authentic aristocrat. Indeed those on the way up were often pathetically eager to ape their betters, and new-fledged gentry could be more aristocratic than the aristocrats in their anxiety to conform to the rules of county life or the etiquette of the London season. This, rather than any fresh breath of counting-house efficiency blowing through the countryside, seems to have been the predominant contribution of the new men; a contribution that strengthened the influence of the landed elite at the same time that it watered down its lineage.[20] The significance of this factor depends, however, on the scale of the process of founding landed families out of industrial and commercial fortunes, and here it is prudent not to be carried away by the impressive lists of new gentry which can undoubtedly be compiled. What is needed is an aggregative measure of the flow, and successive editions of Burke's *Landed Gentry* may serve the purpose. The physical bulk of this register of the untitled landed families roughly doubled between the first edition of 1846 and the 1906 edition. This, however, signified something less than a doubling in the number of individual entries as the habit of maximizing pedigree display caught on and the average length of an entry increased. Moreover, in the years when *Burke* was establishing itself as a social authority, inclusion in which guaranteed even if it did not actually confer gentry status, there was growing pressure from families to get into its pages, with the result that the new entries included many old-established gentry, mainly lesser gentry who had lain neglected in their counties on the first appearance of what perhaps was regarded as a kind of court and high society manual. New entries relating to newly founded families were thus considerably fewer than the doubling of *Burke*'s bulk would imply; and even some of these related to families that had been established by fortunate younger sons of the nobility or existing gentry, and hence were only "new" in a technical sense. A rather rough impression is that not more than a fifth to a quarter of the Edwardian landed gentry were genuinely new men of the captains-of-industry variety, that is to say, under a thousand families.[21]

This impression of the comparative smallness of the new flow, both in relation to the size of the older-established landed class and in relation to the likely number of large fortunes made in industry, trade, banking, and the professions during Victoria's reign, tends to be confirmed by the matter of armorial bearings. Possession of a coat of arms, or its acquisition from the College of Heralds by new men, often to the accompaniment of the manufacture of an appropriate family pedigree, was the best evidence of membership in the landed class, and men paid an annual tax for the privilege of exhibiting this. The higher tax was levied for the most upper-class type of display, armorial bearings emblazoned on the doors of private carriages. It can be assumed that everyone of the highest social standing indulged in the practice, though it must be admitted that some doubt is thrown either on their fiscal reliability or on the sensitivity of the Inland Revenue's social acumen by the violent changes in the numbers of armorial taxpayers that accompanied major changes in the tax. Thus in the first period of constant duties the number of carriages in Britain licensed to carry arms grew from around 20,000 in 1830 to a peak of 24,000 in 1841, and then settled down at around 22,000 until 1853, when the basis of assessment was altered. The number plunged to 12,000 in 1855, and then climbed steadily to 15,000 by 1868, when Gladstonian finance altered the duties again. This change proved more permanent, and under this two-guinea-a-year regime the number of carriages, after a single leap, declined steadily from 19,000 in 1870 to 14,000 in 1900.[22] These figures are difficult to interpret precisely, since they relate to separate carriages and not to individual carriage-owning families, and hence the two-carriage and multi-carriage family was counted several times. There is moreover some evidence that multi-carriage ownership was spreading among the wealthiest families at least until railway facilities had become fully developed, and this would suggest an explanation for the downturn after 1870. By the 1880s, for example, the London and North Western Railway was providing a regular service throughout the shooting season of a horse and carriage special from Euston to the Highlands overnight, and this continued to run until 1914: the very epitome of high Victorian and Edwardian culture, and a useful economizer on private carriage fleets.[23]

The fluctuations of armorial bearings, therefore, appear to be consistent with an upper class with a fairly stable size of something like 12,000 to 15,000 families, tiny in relation to the population at large but large in relation to the likely number of newcomers. Rather different conclusions are suggested by the more humble displays of quarterings, on writing paper or on the family silver and cutlery for instance, for these too attracted the tax man. The number of such licences seems to have grown, with similar breaks in duty rates and assessments, from 7,000 in 1830 to 17,000 in 1853; from 25,000 in 1855 to 43,000 in 1868; and from 39,000 in 1870 to 41,000 in 1900. An early Victorian rush to gentility appears to have been followed by a veritable mid-Victorian stampede, and a late Victorian pause.[24] Clearly such coats of arms were much more widely spread than those of the carriage-folk, and even when allowance is made for the fact that junior branches of the nobility, baronetage, and gentry came within the group, not merely families in the senior line, the totals suggest a massive influx of large cohorts of new men. The diverging trends in armed carriages and crested cutlery present something of a puzzle, to which it is rash to offer a definite solution. But the explanation may well be that the armed carriages reflected the inner group of the upper class, the true elite, which by and large remained possessed of landed estates and all their trappings; while the crested cutlery represented the efforts of the much larger group, particularly of new men, to identify themselves with the Establishment by acquiring some of the less expensive and nonlanded marks of superior status.

The founding of new landed families in the nineteenth century, therefore, is to be viewed as a traditional process continuing within a traditional social structure, rather than as anything strikingly new either in character or in scale. The novel feature was an acceleration in the speed of social absorption and acquisition of gentry status, not a growth or multiplication of the propensity to buy land. Until the early years of Victoria the social acclimatization of new gentry had generally taken two, or even three, generations. The first generation, the maker of the family fortune and the founder of its estate, had been too closely identified with business and profit-making to be capable of making the transition, late in life, to the different values of a country gentleman. County society would usually baulk at such a gritty pebble, but would accept the son or grandson, who had the right kind of upbringing, and who stood a good chance of becoming a J.P. Only the exceptional new man was socially recognized in his own lifetime at this period: the first Sir Robert Peel, whose estate purchasing was vast enough to get him into Parliament for his Tamworth seat; or Sir Richard Arkwright, who gained a knighthood from rising to be sheriff of Derbyshire. In the middle and later nineteenth century, however, it became increasingly normal for the wealthy industrialist turned landowner to receive instant acceptance into the habits and homes of the landed elite. This happened, we have seen, to Charles Tennant with his fortune from the Glasgow chemical works and astute speculative dealings in metals, mining shares, and Australian land, his 4,000 acre estate purchased in 1852, and his baronetcy in 1885; and to James Campbell, father of Campbell-Bannerman, with his Glasgow fortune, his 4,000 acre estate in Forfar, and his knighthood. Many other examples might be cited. From the iron and steel industry came John Guest, the Dowlais ironmaster, already well on his way to acceptance with his 1838 baronetcy before he purchased the 12,000 acre Canford estate in 1845; and Lowthian Bell of the Middlesborough iron trade progressed rapidly to a North Riding estate, an expensively fashionable new country house at Rounton Grange, and a baronetcy in 1885. In engineering and armaments, William Armstrong's Elswick works on Tyneside yielded a large estate in Northumberland, the fantastic Norman Shaw house of Cragside on it, a knighthood, and a barony in 1887. In textiles, Samuel Cunliffe-Lister made an immense fortune out of wool-combing, eventually built up an estate of over 34,000 acres in Yorkshire, and acquired a peerage as Lord Masham in 1891; while Thomas Coats of the Paisley sewing-thread firm acquired a smaller estate, in Renfrew, and then a baronetcy in 1894. A newer industry, cigarette making, threw up its giant firm W. D. & H. O. Wills, and two Willses promptly received baronetcies, the son of W. D. in 1893 and the son of H. O. in 1897 shortly after estate-making exercises in Somerset and Hampshire. Whisky, in the person of John Haig of Cameron Bridge, Fife, J.P. was content with the more modest advance of a place in the *Landed Gentry* and the uncertain future glory of fathering Field Marshal Douglas Haig.[25]

Advance in the span of a single generation from business office to membership of the bench or better thus became well-established practice. That it did so meant that the landed elite became noticeably more open in its reception of new blood than it had been formerly, even if it did not receive significantly larger quantities. The key to the survival of the landed elite, and to its partial transformation, may indeed lie in the question of openness and accessibility rather than in the admission charges and rates applied to nonlanded wealth directly seeking landed status. High society, though conducted by the aristocracy in its town and country houses and regulated by the ruling titled hostesses of the day, had never been completely exclusive in the sense of confining the circle of invitations, receptions, soirees, conversaziones, dinners, balls, shooting parties, hunting parties, or country-house weekends entirely to fellow members of the landed class, whether their status was old established or newly gotten. The question is whether it became less exclusive in the nineteenth century. One side in society dispensed invitations and thus were the arbiters of inclusion or exclusion: these in the main were people, quite largely women, of established position and wealth, grandees by birth or grandees by fashion. The other side accepted, but through insufficient wealth or position were generally unable to reciprocate: these were the men and women of no family

but with claims to recognition either through the utility of their connections and specialized professional knowledge and skills, or through
their distinction in beauty, wit, culture, or sheer entertainment value.
The receivers might indeed become powerful enough, through the
direct enjoyment of aristocratic patronage or later in the century
through reputations boosted more indirectly by aristocratic associations, to control questions of taste and fashion in art, literature, architecture, or dress. The semiautonomy of an artistic elite, however, was
compatible with its existence under the loosely exercised suzerainty of
a superior landed elite: indeed such a relationship is central to the
argument that the aristocratic embrace was more important in win-
ning friends and followers than in leading to the marriage bed.[26]

What did society encompass besides an artistic group? Society as it
existed in Victoria's early years can be conveniently delineated
through the collection of drawings of society personalities by the
Count d'Orsay. For twenty years after 1831 he and the countess of
Blessington "wielded a sort of supremacy over a considerable circle of
the artistic and fashionable world of London."[27] All the celebrities of
the time called at Gore House in Kensington, where the countess held
court, and one by one they went into her lover's sketchbook; the best
of them even went on to the open market when reproduced and
published as engravings. Besides members of the nobility, well-known
hunting squires, and orthodox politicians, the list included a stray
Radical, Thomas Duncombe the M.P. who presented the 1842 Chartist
petition, whom society was no doubt curious to inspect at close quarters and possibly to tame; there were contingents of the inevitable
admirals, generals, and diplomats; there were authors, painters, a poet
or two, and Richard Westmacott the sculptor; and John Gardner
Wilkinson, explorer and Egyptologist, who received a knighthood for
his contributions in 1839. Beyond these spheres of political, literary,
and artistic interest the only person from the business world who
seems to have been socially knowable was Richard Tattersall, the
horse auctioneer.[28] Tattersall was no doubt aptly chosen, representing
precisely that section of commerce which catered for the consuming
and eminently aristocratic passion for horse racing and hunting.

Thirty or forty years later, in the 1880s, society had begun to
change, but the lowering of barriers was so tentative and recent that it
excited sharp comment. Punch, for example, poked fun at the self-
made man struggling to drop the correct number of g's when talking
to a duchess about the humiliations of mixin' with a grocer's wife at
dinner and shootin' with some haberdasher down in the country, only
to discover that the duchess was the daughter of a tradesman in any

case.[29] The earl of Aberdeen, himself a considerable figure on the
Whig side of the elite, recalled in his autobiography that society in the
1870s and 1880s was the large landowners, whose wives and daughters
attended the queen's drawing rooms while they themselves went to
the levees. "Nobody could come to the front without participating in
the London Season," he said, "it was the elite of the governing classes,"
and then proceeded to outline the underlying timetable of society.
First came the pre-Easter season, from the opening of Parliament to
April, when there were political receptions, dinners, small dances, and
political evening parties. From Easter to the end of July was the high
season, the time for the big society events, state balls, concerts at the
palace, balls at the great town houses, and outdoor occasions like
Derby Day and Ascot. In the late season came the garden parties—
only rarely at the palace, though quite often the Prince of Wales gave
one at Marlborough House—"and you had to be seen at Holland
House, Sion House, Argyll Lodge, and Osterley Park to be anyone."
Besides the large landowners, Lord Aberdeen recalled that the top
civil servants, a few select London residents, and a few literary people
did the season; but "the appearance of captains of industry and local
magnates at a Society function would still excite comment."[30] A few
had nevertheless begun to appear, and Lord Aberdeen himself might
be held to have contributed a little to the process when he married the
younger daughter of Dudley Coutts Marjoribanks, partner in Coutts
and Company, bankers to the nobility, though also first Lord
Tweedsmouth. Several of the few were politicians, who gained admit-
tance on the strength of their political importance. The screw manufacturer from Birmingham, Joseph Chamberlain, may be reckoned one
of these; his red-hot radicalism, almost too much for Gladstone, did
not unfit him for the aristocratic embrace of Lady Dorothy Nevill.
Others noticed by the society paper of the time, *Vanity Fair*, included
Michael Thomas Bass, the Burton brewer and M.P., of whom it
wrote: "There is now a class of politicians who seek to suppress vice
and misery by removing the comforts of the poor . . . by legislating
the ruled many into the condition of smug-faced teadrinkers . . . Mr
Bass represents one of the great ramparts against this new oppression.
. . . His name is known in every quarter of the world; it is daily spoken
in remote spots where the names of Gladstone and Disraeli, of Lowe
and Grenville, have never been heard, and it will be remembered with
gratitude when they are utterly forgotten."[31] So it has proved; his son
is perhaps less clearly recalled as the first beer baron—he was created
Lord Burton in 1886. There were also nonpolitical figures from the
business world, such as James Brand, "the Telephone," who was a

popular and welcome figure in society in the 1880s, a keen member of Brooks's and the Coaching Club, often seen driving his drag round his place at Sanderstead Court. He was the head of a leading house in the China trade, Harvey, Brand and Company, but was chiefly known for his promotion of telephones, being largely responsible for the commercial success of the early London telephone companies.[32] Industrialists and businessmen were being filtered into society, slowly and selectively.

The social sieve became decidedly coarser from the 1890s onwards, so that by the time of Edwardian society rules and exclusiveness alike had been much relaxed. On the one hand those with literary and intellectual interests tried to counter the triviality and boredom of the old formal social round by introducing some liveliness, as in the deep conversations and intellectual parlor games of the group of young society starlets known as the Souls; or by admitting people from the stage, like Mrs Langtry or Beerbohm Tree, which was scarcely permissible before the 1890s. On the other hand those who were impressed by wealth and ostentation opened the doors of society more and more freely regardless of origins or breeding, in the interests of ever more extravagant displays of food and drink, costume and jewellery, indoor and outdoor sport. The second influence was the predominant one. This became the age of the South African millionaires with their gold and diamond fortunes, the Randlords as they were called, of Alfred Beit, and Sir Julius Wernher; of the international financier Sir Ernest Cassel; and of the grocery-chain proprietor Sir Thomas Lipton. All these, though not precisely captains of industry, were at ease in Edwardian society; and Wernher for one, purchasing one place of authentically aristocratic lineage in town, Bath House, and another in the country at Luton Hoo, performed as host in magnificent style at enormous expense. Luton Hoo alone, with its staff of fifty-four gardeners, ten electricians, and twenty or thirty house servants, was said to cost £30,000 a year to keep up.[33] Many have criticized Edwardian society for conspicuous consumption of champagne, and strawberries and cream, for waste and futility; but it should not therefore be concluded that it was a society of vulgar millionaires— and Wernher himself, with his art collection and his interest in scientific education, was not vulgar—rather than a society which accepted vulgar millionaires into its circle. In truth Edwardian society remained in the hands of the traditional elite, and at the top it meant Mrs George Keppel, Edward VII's favorite mistress, a great beauty, and though untitled nevertheless married to the brother of the earl of Albemarle; it meant Millicent, duchess of Sutherland, another beauty and one of the Souls in the 1890s; it meant Mrs George Cornwallis-West, widow of Lord Randolph Churchill, a New York girl whose second husband was a cousin of the Earl De La Warr; and it meant the Rothschilds—Nathan Meyer, the first baron, and his brother Alfred —great bankers, great landowners, and great entertainers of Edward VII.[34] There was indeed some infusion of new blood among these society leaders; more accurately, perhaps, one could say that a certain amount of new wine had been poured into old bottles, and the bottles had not cracked.

The landed elite, particularly its central manifestation in London society, was so successful in accommodating, absorbing, and containing the various thrusts and pressures generated in the world outside the landed estates largely because no counter-elite emerged to challenge it. It is perfectly true, of course, that there were always many other elite groups in the provinces, in different communities of residence, religion, or skill, and that these became stronger, more defined, and more closely knit in the course of the century with the development of organizations and institutions. Whether these were chambers of commerce, employers' associations, trade unions, or professional organizations, they all tended to define spheres of activity for elites. Even without formal organization a literary elite, an artistic elite, or an intellectual elite could perfectly well be identified in the early nineteenth century, though the existence of the Royal Academy and the Society of Painters and Sketchers helps in the task. Such elites, and equally those of Dissenting chapels or the medical profession, certainly owed nothing to any landowning membership and very little to influences of the landed elite exercised from without. They were characterized, however, by their limited and functional outlook; they were the cream of their own community, and their purpose was to regulate it and defend, explain, or represent it to the outside world. Their existence did not imply any ambition to dispute issues of wider control and influence with the landed elite. Only once in the nineteenth century was there a possibility of an antielite, with a class basis, and that was when the leaders of the Anti-Corn Law League were poised for a general attack on the aristocratic monopoly. Even then the width of the objectives in administrative, political, and social reconstruction probably vastly exceeded the width of support, so that the rapid collapse after 1846 of any prospect of a middle-class elite peddling a general bourgeois ethic comes as little surprise. The salami technique of the upper class, nibbling away at these other elites by taking them into the charmed circle, was much more reliable.

The ecclesiastical elite is an excellent example of a group of top people that remained part and parcel of the Establishment, the flying buttress of the aristocracy as it were, even while its links with the great landowners grew weaker. At Victoria's accession the church was still very much what the eighteenth century had made it. The recruitment of the clergy was in the hands of the landowners who controlled presentations to livings, and birth and upbringing counted above all in defining the field. The church's elite, the bench of bishops, was still a small group of twenty-six—and tightly knit at any rate in its view of the 1831 Reform Bill—that formed a strong branch of the aristocracy. About half the bishops were of noble birth, while the other half had been private tutors to the aristocracy. The system of presentation had not greatly altered by the end of the nineteenth century, but it was no longer used to any great extent to advance either political or family interests—education and doctrinal position having filled the place vacated by support for gentlemen's sons as the keys to patronage. The episcopacy, swollen by the creation of new industrial sees and the appointment of suffragans, had grown into a body of sixty, of whom scarcely a quarter were of aristocratic birth; something approaching one-half the bishops were sons of clergymen, indicating the dynastic tendencies of the liberal professions. But if the late Victorian bishops were increasingly nonaristocratic in origin they showed aristocratic tastes once their careers were launched. Of those who married— nearly 90 percent of the group—half found wives who came from aristocratic or landed gentry families, while less than one-third of the wives were clergymen's daughters. The rest of the bishops and their wives came from professional backgrounds, the armed services, the colonial service, the law, and medicine; there is not a trace of trade or industry, perhaps because such families could hardly comprehend religion as a proper living. In other words this was an elite that, although by no means immune to change, had scarcely begun to cast off its traditional ties or to modify its traditional role as an adjunct of aristocracy.[35]

There were, of course, many more men of ability and ambition than could be incorporated into the sphere of the landed elite simply by giving social recognition to the most eminent or the most wealthy. The larger pool beyond was, however, within reach of the attractions of the public service and the operations of the honors system. Hereditary honors, peerages and baronetages, had always been supposed to be accompanied by a landed estate adequate to support the dignity of the title. Until the 1880s this convention—which might be held to have stipulated about £2,000 a year from land for a peerage and £500 a year for a baronetcy—was pretty well maintained. One or two generals and

Alfred Lord Tennyson seem to have been the only exceptions made.[36] Even Edward Strutt, hailed in 1856 as the first industrialist to be given a peerage, was no exception. The *Manchester Examiner* might comment that "it is as a manufacturer, and to mark the interest which the Queen takes in the manufacturing pursuits of the country that Mr Strutt is metamorphosed into Baron Belper. As such it is a graceful and a prudent act. It shows a wise appreciation of the signs of the times. It is something for those who claim to be regarded as the descendants of the mailed barons of England to admit into their order, a man who has not only made but is making his fortune by spindles and looms."[37] Strutt, however, was the third generation in the family business, had been educated at Trinity College Cambridge, had a rich country estate of 5,000 acres, had been an M.P. for twenty-five years, and had held office: not a typical industrialist. The change came in the 1880s, with the beer and stout of Allsopp, Guinness, and Bass floating the peerages of Hindlip, Ardilaun, Iveagh, and Burton. Between 1886 and 1914 some 200 individuals entered the peerage for the first time, only about half of them coming from families with landed backgrounds. About 70 of them were industrialists, merchants, or bankers; and though half of this group had acquired country estates, the other half had not. This was a radical departure; though it must be remembered that 35 or so nonlanded industrialist peers would not make a great deal of impression on the 570-strong House of Lords.[38]

The fate of the nonhereditary honors is perhaps more significant, for these could always be bestowed on men of distinction in public life without any reservations about the capacity of successors to maintain a style of life fitting to the dignity. The chief of these were knighthoods, either in specified orders, of which the Order of the Bath was the most ancient, or unadorned knights bachelor. Knights and their ladies were certainly persons of consequence, and the title gave them if not automatic entry into London society at any rate a definite position in the social hierarchy and a place in the reflected glory of the landed elite. The utility of the awards is illustrated by the creation of fresh orders of knighthood each with its own kind of exclusiveness. The Prince Regent in romantic mood created the Royal Hanoverian Guelphic Order in 1815, though this had to be discontinued in 1837 when the crowns of Britain and Hanover separated. He also established the Order of St Michael and St George in 1818. The needs of India produced the Star of India in 1861 and the Order of the Indian Empire in 1878; while the rapid expansion of meritorious aspects of public life furnished the Royal Victorian Order in 1896. The structure was not completed until 1917, with the institution of the Order of the

British Empire, destined to become the largest and most frequently
used honor of them all. How was this machinery of honors employed?
At Victoria's accession there were about 650 knights all told, and by
1885 the total had grown very little, to about 700. Proportions had
changed. In 1840 there were 200 knights of the named orders and
450 knights bachelor; in 1885 the position was reversed, 470 in orders
and 230 bachelors. The orders were generally reserved for service in
specific fields, such as diplomacy, war, Indian government, colonial
administration, and the home civil service; while those whose distinction grew in more miscellaneous spheres tended to be made knights
bachelor. The change therefore suggests that the opportunities for
industrialists, men of letters, scientists, and the like can hardly have
been increasing dramatically between 1840 and 1885. By 1914, however, the knightage had topped 1,700, with 1,000 in the orders and 700
bachelors, a doubling of the first category and trebling of the second.[39]

This great expansion points, as do all the other indicators, to the
years after the 1880s as the period of real change. But does it point to
decisive change? The kind of service or eminence which earned
knighthoods did not alter much. Of the knights who were alive in
1882, 84 percent had gained their honors by some kind of public and
official service: they were generals, admirals, colonial governors, Indian civil servants, diplomats, civil servants, lord mayors, sheriffs,
mayors, local government leaders, or just plain politicians. The proportion in 1912 was 79 percent, practically unchanged. What may be
called professional service—in law, medicine, religion, arts and music,
science, the universities, engineering, architecture, publishing, explor-
ing, and the like—accounted for 14 percent of the 1882 knights and 17
percent of the 1912 force, leaving the commercial sector of agriculture, industry, transport, and trade with a mere 9 knights in 1882, 1.4
percent of the total, and 64 knights in 1912, 3.6 percent of the total.
Some industrialists, indeed, earned knighthoods for public services;
and while only 9 manufacturing knights have been counted in the
commercial category, 14 more manufacturers can be identified in the
public service sector. It is more than likely that a high proportion of
the knighted lord mayors and mayors were prominent local businessmen, industrialists in disguise as it were; there were 51 of them in 1882
and 144 in 1912, but even if they were all deemed to belong properly
to the commercial category it would not greatly modify the impression of overall official dominance of the knightage.[40]

The social and family backgrounds of the knights are of as much
importance as the nature of their careers, but here the information

disclosed by each knight in his potted biography might well have been fuller. No indication at all is given of father's status or occupation in 32 percent of the cases in 1882 and 47 percent in 1912. In the remainder, where indications are given of father's title, rank, occupation, or standing, the traditional backgrounds predominated much as one would expect, since a man would be pleased to lay claim to them. Thus 82 percent in 1882 and 85 percent in 1912 came from traditional families and had fathers who were peers, baronets, knights, landed gentlemen, military or naval officers, civil servants, or Anglican clergymen. By contrast only eighteen individuals, in both years, actually stated that their fathers were in business or trade. Even if the extreme assumption is made that all those fathers with no stated occupation were businessmen or something more humble, it still leaves about half the knights of both years with social origins within the orbit of the landed class. Something like this may well be near the mark; it implies a wide channel of upward social mobility carrying the cream of the industrial and professional middle classes into at least the lower reaches of the upper-class elite. The fact that the relative size of this channel remained virtually unchanged between 1882 and 1912, though the absolute size of the knightly group almost trebled, implies an all-round enlargement of the opportunities for earning knighthoods rather than any pronounced alteration in the recruiting grounds for knights.

It all comes down to the far-flung empire in the end, which of course was being vigorously flung precisely in the years after 1882. This was where the knighthoods were chiefly won, and in this and its allied spheres of the armed forces, diplomacy, and the tasks of keeping home administration ticking over, lay the main interests of the state. Looking after these affairs was what high politics was all about, the high politics of place, position, and maneuvre that it was the function of the landed elite to conduct. The sons of the wealthier middle classes, groomed in the public schools and at Oxford and Cambridge, came forth to join the sons of the vicarages and the country houses in performing the business of government in the field and in the office. These were the state's men of business, successors perhaps on a wider stage to the sixteenth-century justices of the peace. They were the working professionals, the players, and by playing they accepted the rules of the game laid down by the gentlemen, the game of high politics. The ablest and luckiest of them were knighted, and thus were seen to have joined the gentlemen, becoming attached to the ruling elite by title as well as by service. Alongside this solid phalanx, strengthening and in no way challenging the landed leaders, was the small number of industrialists who were knighted—like Sir Henry Bessemer, the steel manufacturer, in 1879; Sir Hiram Maxim, the inventor of the maxim gun, in 1901; or the completely unremembered motor manufacturer Sir Charles Hain Friswell in 1909—or railwaymen such as Sir Henry Oakley, the general manager of the Great Northern knighted in 1891; and Sir James Inglis, general manager of the Great Western knighted in 1911. This small number represented no more than an occasional drop of oil serving to keep the social machine running sweetly and without friction.

In these several ways, through the absorption of new wealth, control of social recognition and acceptance, continued domination of high society, judicious exploitation of the aristocratic embrace, and cultivation of the honors system and the public service, the machine kept running and the gentry's rules were observed in playing the game. It changed not through the players overpowering the gentlemen, but when the rules of high politics changed. Before 1914 the business of government was not much concerned with internal affairs, with material questions, with class interests, or was only just beginning to be so. The needs of total war followed by an economy turned upside down altered all that. When the business of government, and hence of high politics, became concerned with the sheer survival of the nation, with the life and death of individuals and the life and death of businesses, everyone wishing to take part had to become professionals, players all. It was then that the members of the old landed elite who could not or would not turn pro retired to the pavilion to watch and to mutter that they could have managed better than the new lot.

NOTES

1. Lord Hawke, "The Story of the M.C.C.," *The M.C.C. 1787–1937* (London: *The Times*, 1937), pp. 9–10.
2. See, for example, C. L. Mowat, *Britain between the Wars, 1918–1940* (1955), pp. 148–49, 397; Patrick Balfour, *Society Racket* (1932), p. 125; Margaret I. Cole, ed., *Beatrice Webb's Diaries, 1912–1924* (1952), pp. 236–37, 263; and O. F. Christie, *The Transition to Democracy, 1867–1914* (1934), p. 251.
3. W. L. Guttsman, ed., *The English Ruling Class* (1969), introduction and documents 2.10, 3.16, 4.15; Christie, *The Transition*, pp. 275–301.
4. "Is Society Worse Than It Was?", *Nineteenth Century* (1903). Esme Wingfield-Stratford, *Before the Lamps Went Out* (1945), pp. 230–35.
5. H. J. Hanham, *Elections and Party Management* (1959).
6. W. L. Guttsman, *The British Political Elite* (1963), pp. 90, 104.
7. Recalculated from Neal Blewett, *The Peers, the Parties and the People: The General Election of 1910* (1972), p. 230. Blewett states that there were 610 Liberal

candidates in the two elections, but the subtotals in his table of occupations appear to total 607.

8. Guttsman, *British Political Elite*, pp. 36–38.

9. *Burke's Landed Gentry* (1871), 1: 306; J. Bateman, *The Great Landowners of Great Britain and Ireland* (1878), p. 2; Viscount Chilston, *W. H. Smith* (1965).

10. Guttsman, *British Political Elite*, p. 83.

11. *Return of Owners of Lands and Heritages, Scotland, 1872–3* (C.899, 1874), s. v. "Sir James Campbell of Strathcathro, Breckin, Co. Forfar"; Roy Jenkins, *Asquith* (1964), pp. 13–16.

12. Mark Bonham Carter, ed., *The Autobiography of Margot Asquith* (1962), p. xxiii.

13. Ibid., pp. xxi, 199.

14. Ibid., pp. 155, 208.

15. *Burke's Peerage and Baronetage* (1936), p. 1841.

16. Jenkins, *Asquith*, pp. 271–72.

17. R. J. Minney, *"Puffin" Asquith* (1970).

18. *The Economist*, 5 Jan. 1867.

19. Ibid., 29 June 1850; 16 July 1870.

20. A different view is expressed in J. T. Ward and R. G. Wilson, eds., *Land and Industry* (1971), although this chiefly relates to the late eighteenth century and appears in the contributions of R. G. Wilson, "The Denisons and Milneses: Eighteenth-century Merchant Landowners," and T. M. Devine, "Glasgow Colonial Merchants and Land, 1770–1815."

21. J. Bateman's tables, "County Tables of Landowners," in George C. Brodrick, *English Land and English Landlords* (1881) show a total of around 4,200 landowners of gentry proportions [owning over 1,000 acres] in England and Wales, including the peerage. If Scotland is added, this produces a little under 5,000 landed gentry in Britain in 1873, a figure consistent with the total entries in *Burke's Landed Gentry* (1871) which included the Irish gentry. Hence it seems that the *Burke* entries, though resting on social status rather than simple estate ownership, corresponded closely to the facts of ownership. The 1906 edition of *Burke* contains rather over 5,000 entries, again including Irish gentry, and a count under surnames beginning with the letters *A* and *S* suggests that between 20 and 25 percent relate to families that acquired their estates in the course of the nineteenth century. Not all of these newcomers derived their fortunes from industry, commerce, or banking; and an unknown proportion may well have acquired their estates by inheritance rather than purchase. The information given in *Burke* is by no means uniform or precise, and more detailed research could well render the present tentative conclusion out of date.

22. *Thirteenth Report of the Commissioners of Inland Revenue*, Parliamentary Papers, 1870, XX, "Assessed Taxes. Schedule K, Armorial Bearings," p. 179; *Twenty-fourth Report of the Commissioners of Inland Revenue*, P.P. 1881, XXIX, "Armorial Bearings Licences," p. 367. After 1889 armorial bearings, along with other licences, were made part of the "Establishment Licences" whose proceeds were handed over to local authorities; the annual totals were recorded in editions of *Whitaker's Almanack*.

23. C. L. Mowat, "The Heyday of the British Railway System: Vanishing Evidence and the Historian's Task," *Journal of Transport History*, n.s. 1 (1971).

24. *Thirteenth Rep. Commrs. Inland Revenue; Twenty-Fourth Rep. Commrs. Inland Revenue; Whitaker's Almanack.* There were major changes in the basis of assessment in 1853 and 1868, as well as rather more frequent changes in rates of duty, so that the series in the Inland Revenue returns are not comparable over the whole century. The categories used by the Revenue authorities are so briefly described that there is not sufficient information to attempt any splices at the changeovers. In the text, therefore, the raw figures are used. They are rounded and assigned to categories that correspond roughly with the Revenue's terminology.

25. *Burke's Landed Gentry* (1871 and 1906 eds.); *Burke's Peerage, Baronetage and Knightage* (1902); *Autobiography of Margot Asquith*; Earl of Bessborough, ed., *The Diaries of Lady Charlotte Guest* (1950).

26. The data on the marriage partners of sons and daughters of peers given by T. H. Hollingsworth (*The Demography of the British Peerage*, Supplement to *Population Studies* 18 (1964): 8–10 and table 1) convey the opposite impression, i.e., that the marrying of nonnoble blood, having been very stable in the eighteenth century, began to become more frequent from the early nineteenth century and very much more frequent from about 1880 onwards. This last change undoubtedly reflects a real social transformation, not merely in the marriage partners of peers' children but also in the social composition of the peerage itself. For earlier periods, however, it is necessary to remember that Hollingsworth employs only two social categories for sorting out marriage partners, "noble" and "common," and that they form an analytical instrument that contemporary society would have regarded as excessively blunt since by implication the daughters and sons of the untitled landed gentry, the clergy, and the armed services have been classed as being as "common" as tradesmen's children. In other words, without further refinement Hollingsworth's data do not say very much about the marriage habits of the landed aristocracy.

27. *Dictionary of National Biography*, s. v. "Alfred Guillaume Gabriel, Count d'Orsay."

28. National Portrait Gallery, Count Alfred d'Orsay collection, "Men About Town, 1832–48."

29. *Punch*, 12 May 1888, p. 219; 9 June 1888, p. 274; 4 Aug. 1888, p. 58.

30. Marquis of Aberdeen, *More Cracks with "We Twa"* (1929), pp. 5–9.

31. *Vanity Fair*, 20 May 1871.

32. Ibid., 26 May 1888.

33. Beatrice Webb, *Our Partnership* (1948), p. 413.

34. Balfour, *Society Racket*, pp. 47–48, 52.

35. *Burke's Peerage, Baronetage and Knightage* (1902).

36. F. M. L. Thompson, *English Landed Society in the Nineteenth Century* (1963), pp. 51–63.

37. *Manchester Examiner*, quoted by R. E. Pumphrey in "The Introduction of Industrialists into the British Peerage: a Study in Adaptation of a Social Institution," *American Historical Review* 65 (1959).

38. Thompson, *English Landed Society*, pp. 292–97.

39. Knights in the orders of knighthood and knights bachelor have been taken from the *Royal Kalendar* for 1840 and from *Whitaker's Almanack* for 1885 and 1914.

40. The analysis is based on *Lodge's Peerage and Baronetage* (1882 and 1912 eds.), in which the biographical information on knights is perhaps a little fuller than in *Burke*. In any event until a year by year search of honors lists is undertaken the reasons for obtaining honors have to be inferred from the recipient's career and office.

3 | Prussia

To discuss the landed and nonlanded elites of Germany—or of any other country—in the nineteenth century is a daunting enterprise. Does it exclude anything that is of historical interest? Does it not rather include everything that we would want to know about Germany of the time—and that nineteenth-century Germans themselves grappled with? The relations of the older elite to the new elites of the nineteenth century touch on every aspect of Germany's political, economic, social, and cultural history of the period. In nineteenth-century Europe industrial capitalism transformed existing class relations, but in Germany it did so in a significantly different manner than elsewhere. The triumph of industrialization in the economic realm and the simultaneous bolstering of a preindustrial political and social order have often been identified as the key elements of Germany's unique and uneven development.[1]

Throughout the century, great minds sought to understand the nature of the new society—both what it was and what it should be: Kant and Hegel; Goethe, Börne, and Heine; Stahl and Marx; Bismarck; and finally Fontane, Max Weber, and Thomas Mann. Their works reflect the upheavals of the century and helped mold society's response to these upheavals. The sorrows of young Werther or the fate of Effi Briest's lover are as much a part of this topic as are the fluctuations of grain prices and the changes in landownership. The charm of the topic—aside from its elusiveness—is its implicit reminder that history compartmentalized is history distorted.

In seeking a possible focus for this inquiry, I was reminded of Frederick the Great's exclamation at the battle of Kolin in 1757 when he turned to his men and said: "Rascals, would you live forever?" History put that question to the old Prussian nobility as well, and their answer—repeated for well over a century—was an historic "yes," a yes that exuded defiance of a new era in world history. In my remarks

I shall focus on the Prussian nobility—more precisely, on the East Elbian Junkers because they embodied what might be called the military-agrarian complex of German society. "The historical record," Alexander Gerschenkron wrote, "contains few elite groups endowed with a similar ability to survive."[2]

By a mixture of tenacity and adaptability, the Junkers survived the disappearance of their world. Their refusal to recognize that "the objective conditions of society" had destined them for the dustbin of history would evoke admiration if their stubbornness had not been so costly. Despite the weakening of their economic base after 1873, the Junkers continued until 1914—and beyond—to have a profound impact on the shaping of German society and politics, on the administration of the state and the army, on the ethos of an entire people. For much of the nineteenth century, the Prussian nobility was *tonangebend*: it set the fashion of thought and aspiration for the rest of upper and official society. In fact, the Junker influence broadened as other classes emulated them, and in that way their social power was greater, or at least more pervasive, in the nineteenth century, when they were beset by rivals, than in the eighteenth, when Frederick II assigned them a preeminent place in his army and bureaucracy. The Junker determination to survive, to defy or bend new forces to their interest, to avoid prudential sacrifices of the kind that were made on the night of August 4th, marked the course of German history. Their success can be measured in part by a very simple comparison: in his extraordinary work *France, 1848–1945*, Theodore Zeldin could say with perfect plausibility: "Bourgeois values were thus not just bourgeois. Other classes could also claim at least some of them as their own. Had the aristocracy and the workers believed in radically different ways of life, there would have been far more conflict between the classes. But the bourgeoisie's moderation meant that they consciously or unconsciously represented the common denominator of the ambitions of their time. The phrase *la France bourgeoise* was thus a tautology in that to be a bourgeois meant to subscribe to the most general national aspirations."[3] The same could not be said for Prussia—not in 1800, not in 1850, not in 1878, and not in 1900. In fact it could not be said of Germany until Prussia was annihilated. Why not? The answers must be found not only in the tough resourcefulness of the Junker but in the willing subservience of the newly aspiring elites as well.

The strength of the Junkers rested on their preeminent economic and military-bureaucratic role in the Prussian state. For centuries they had lived on their large East Elbian estates. Individually, they had jurisdiction over these estates and over the people working them both before and, to a large extent, after the emancipation of the serfs; collectively, they dominated the agricultural lands of the old provinces of Prussia. For centuries as well, they had a privileged position in the army and at times in the bureaucracy, and by virtue of birth and service they had immediate access to the court.

In the course of the nineteenth century, they had to fend off successive crises, crises caused by market forces and by Prussian reforms, by the rise of competing mercantile classes, and by the spread of inimical ideas. Their greatest success came in the years from 1850 to 1873, when agricultural prices recovered after the postwar low of 1825–6, when small peasant holdings were annexed by them, and when their political condition was newly strengthened by Bismarck, a Junker whom his fellow Junkers distrusted for his revolutionary adaptability. From 1873 to 1898 the Junkers faced economic threats which no longer could be surmounted by economic resourcefulness alone; they fashioned a new method for survival. Their power had always rested on noneconomic as well as economic factors, and they now devised a new strategy: to speak in pseudo-Marxian terms, they rallied the superstructure in order to bolster their base.

It was, however, not only their economic resourcefulness and their political ruthlessness that saved them; they managed to permeate an increasingly modern society, which in its characteristic workaday activities was far removed from the rural world of the Junkers, with their values, both real and putative. Essentially, they not only defended their interests and sought to protect their power but, on a less conscious level, they managed to insinuate their values, their style of life and thought, into a broad segment of the classes whose interests diverged from theirs. They coerced and cajoled—but they also dazzled and divided the aspiring elites. They imposed their increasingly fraudulent self-image on classes and groups that struggled to attain a self-image of their own. It is a curious fact that the antibourgeois sentiment in Europe found its greatest literary expressions in France and Britain—and its greatest social and political expression in Germany. There was no Balzac or Dickens in Germany, but there were groups in German life—from the Junkers to the youth movement— who despised the money-grubbing, repressive, pompously insecure *Bürger*. In capitalist Germany, anticapitalism flourished, and it had its impact on the capitalists themselves. I shall suggest that perhaps the greatest coup of the Junkers was to have their values generally accepted at a time when they themselves, so engrossed in defending their interests, had become less respectful of these values. By the end of the century, after decades of unprecedented economic growth and modernization, Germany was essentially governed by one upper stratum—an uneasy amalgam of different classes and different interests, still subordinated to the pseudoaristocratic values of the past and pledged to the common defense of privilege, which stance was defined as national virtue.

To understand these processes, it would be necessary to deal with the actual conditions of the Junkers and with their changing self-assessment as well as with the development of their rivals and their rivals' self-assessment, and to do both against the background of changing economic and political realities. In what follows I can touch on but a few of these themes.

For centuries the Hohenzollern rulers and the Junkers had maintained a tacit alliance. The Hohenzollerns exercised political authority, while "the nobility became a service nobility; it identified its interests with those of the state which gave it positions of honor and profit."[4] By virtue of this alliance, the Crown ruled the state and the Junkers controlled their estates and their serfs. The alliance, while mutually advantageous, suffered occasional strains. It is well known that the Prussian kings thought their Junkers capable of becoming *frondeurs* and that the Junkers often felt their monarchs to be remiss in their principal duty, which was to favor the preeminent caste of the country.

Frederick the Great had reaffirmed the alliance and had given Prussian nobles a preeminent place in the Prussian officer corps and the Prussian bureaucracy. According to him, the nobility alone embodied honor, and honor was to be the animating virtue of his army and his state. At the end of Frederick's reign, the Prussian nobility enjoyed its old privileges of landholding and patrimonial justice; it enjoyed the new privilege of having the principal claim on the state's positions. The Junkers had no rivals in power, in status, and probably not in wealth; in a poor country, they were still the most prosperous group. Their unique position was formally acknowledged in the Prussian Legal Code of 1794; their identity as a separate estate was defined, both in its privileges and its limits. The limits corresponded to the principle of honor on which depended their moral claims. The Junkers could not enter into bourgeois pursuits, could not sell their knightly estates to nonnobles, could not marry in a manner that would violate their station. The Legal Code, it should be added, confirmed as well the special role of the Prussian bureaucracy; it "granted civil

servants the legal status of a corporative body, complete with rights
and duties separate from those of both the traditional aristocratic and
bourgeois estates. . . . The *Beamtenstand* was recognized as a part of a
select body of privileged individuals who were, in effect, the first
citizens of the state."[5] By recognizing the new "aristocracy of service," it strengthened it. The relations between that bureaucracy and
the older nobility were immensely complicated: the bureaucracy identified itself with the state; the nobility prided itself on its independence and sought to preserve its privilege against the inroads of an arm
of state that contained many of its own class. In his contemptuous
impatience with the bureaucracy, the young Bismarck, himself a
member of the judicial administration, mirrored the view of many of
his fellow Junkers. The Legal Code confirmed the privileges of the
landed and of the service elites—at the very time when the position
of the nobility was being challenged from the most diverse sources.[6]

The great literary and philosophical revival of the late eighteenth
century implicitly questioned the absolutes of the Legal Code. In the
Sturm und Drang beginnings of German idealism, the claims of moral
superiority based on birth were mocked and vilified. Goethe and
Schiller celebrated the rights of individual passion, not of caste privilege. In the 1770s and 1780s they dramatized the glories of becoming,
not the enjoyment of being; they denounced the artificiality of a
society based on birth, not human worth; and generations of Germans
remembered the social-psychic injury that young Werther received at
the hands of caste-conscious nobility. Among *Bürger* of the late eighteenth century there was widespread exasperation with the presump-
tion and violence and freakish tyranny of ruthless nobles. Still, "the
word *fraternité* had no place in the German political vocabulary."[7]

The challenge to the nobility came, however, from more than
philosophers and poets, important though these were. It came with the
doctrines and battalions of a liberated people from across the Rhine;
Frederick's state collapsed on its own chosen field when Prussian
troops dissolved in an ignominious rout before Napoleon's troops. The
Prussian defeat opened the door to reform, and reform needed to
take account of the galvanizing principles of the triumphant adver-
sary. Defeats, like deficits, are often a nation's treasure. The reformers,
who were both Prussian and non-Prussian, noble and nonnoble, were
men of the highest moral and political caliber; their aim was to tran-
scend the "soulless machinery" that Frederick had bequeathed incompetent heirs and, while maintaining a properly ordered monarchical
and deferential society, to create a new mode of life that would release
the fettered energies of the people and bring their voluntary loyalty to

the state. According to the reformers, peasants and army recruits could not be beaten into subservience, talent had to be recognized, and measures of self-government decreed—liberties had to be granted in order to avoid the lure of liberty, which the reformers too thought tantamount to anarchy. In the process of modernizing an antiquated society, the holders of privilege seemed most immediately threatened. Nor did the reformers have an excessively high opinion of the privileged; in 1808 Baron von Stein described the landed aristocracy as "numerous, for the most part poor, and pretentious concerning salary, office, privilege, and benefits of every sort."[8] In the ensuing years the reformers leveled some barriers. In the army and in the bureaucracy, the principle of merit, not birth, as the basis of selections was introduced—with the clear intent that nonnobles should be able to compete with nobles. Commoners were no longer barred from buying noble lands, and nobles could pursue what had hitherto been deemed nonnoble vocations. The division of society into fixed estates ceased; a class society took its place. The peasant was freed from manorial obligations but was obliged to pay for his new independence by ceding some of his land to the landowner. As part of the same reform spirit, and again partly in emulation of certain practical measures of the French Revolution, the Jews of Prussia (or those in the old provinces of Prussia) were emancipated. In short, an effort was made to end or alleviate the conditions of dependency, to end the period of communal passivity, to turn, in the phrase of the day, subject into citizen.

A Junker *fronde*, led by Ludwig von der Marwitz, thundered against these dangerous imports from abroad, which it believed would negate the very principles of order and hierarchy on which Prussia had been raised. Marwitz's opposition to what in 1811 he called the "newfangled Jew state" was frenetic.[9] He sensed in the very notion of a *bürgerliche Gesellschaft* (civil society), which Hegel posited at that very time and which the reforms seemed to approximate, a denial of the special role of the nobility. A nobility that would have to compete on merit for positions in the bureaucracy and the army, a nobility that would have to prove its economic viability by surviving the vicissitudes of the market—such a nobility was condemned to fight for its birthright. In the second and third decade of the nineteenth century, the Junkers worried about their survival, and their critics rejoiced in their anticipated demise. There was much talk about the anachronism of aristocracy; it was sometimes argued that nobles could become the servants of the state but not the masters of society.

Even before the beginnings of reform, the Junkers knew something of economic adversity. By 1800 about ten percent of all noble estates had been sold to nonnobles, and the figure steadily rose, despite the formal interdiction of such alienation.[10] For the rest, the estates were heavily indebted, and the Junkers were not a wealthy elite. The aftermath of the Napoleonic war brought an agrarian crisis; the price of a ton of rye dropped from 7 £ 10s in 1817/8 to 2 £ 16s in 1825/6, which proved the lowest price of the century.[11]

The Junkers survived that first slump and between 1840 and 1873 enjoyed a period of prosperity. They turned to profit the legislation of the Reform Era and the new agricultural opportunities. After the so-called emancipation of the peasants, the peasants' share of the land declined, and the share of the large estates increased dramatically. "Although estates of more than one hundred hectares constituted less than two percent of all holdings in the east, the area under their control rose to forty-two percent." Approximately two and a half million acres of peasant land came into the hands of the large landowner.[12] The Junkers—and those commoners who in increasing measure bought noble land—became ever more adept at modern farming, at increasing production, and at economic management. In the middle decades of the century, prices and production rose dramatically—and still the one danger that haunted many of the Junkers was indebtedness, caused by the efforts at modernizing, by the vicissitudes of the harvest, and by the one vice that Junkers indulged in hoping to escape penury and monotony—gambling. Between 1837 and 1857 the mortgage debts on their properties doubled.[13] Indebtedness may be productive or unproductive; it may finance improvements or postpone the results of mismanagement. To the Junkers it was a worrisome matter, the more so as indebtedness was often the first step on the way to the alienation of land. The Junkers were always afraid that their estates might end up in the hands of commoners, even in the hands of the worst kind of commoners, Jews. (In 1835 there were already fifty-one noble estates in Jewish hands, half of them in Silesia.)[14]

In this middle period, then, the owners of Prussia's large estates became entrepreneurs of the soil. They proved adept at the new task, even as they sometimes insisted that it violated their character and jeopardized their function. As Max Weber put it much later: "The old economic order asked: How can I give, on this piece of land, work and sustenance to the greatest possible number of men? Capitalism asks: From this given piece of land how can I produce as many crops as possible for the market with as few men as possible? . . . Today the landlord acts as any businessman, and he must act thus, but his aristocratic traditions contrast with such action. He would like to be a feudal lord, yet he must become a commercial entrepreneur and a capitalist."[15] Junkers liked to think of themselves as patriarchal rulers on their estates; their psychic satisfactions came overwhelmingly from the sense of property that they experienced; it was *their* fields, *their* forests, *their* hunting grounds, *their* cattle, *their* horses, and above all *their* peasants, their *Leute*, that they embraced when they spoke of their estates. It was here in their daily lives that the inherited habit of authority was exercised and the assumption of superiority confirmed. Would any of them *voluntarily* give up the rural patrimony, the lifted cap of peasant or stable boy for an uncertain career elsewhere? Yet most of them recognized that the demands of managing estates in efficient ways put pressures on them that violated the old patriarchal relations that were at the base not only of peasant contentment but of their own pleasures. Still, the demands of profitability had to take precedence over other considerations. As a class, the Junkers learned rapidly; they adapted themselves to the new demands with extraordinary dexterity and at a cost that they came to realize only much later.

In the process, they became somewhat less parochial, somewhat more integrated into the larger world around them. In 1847 Bismarck complained that "experience has led me away from the delusion about the Arcadian happiness of a landowner incarnate, with double-entry bookkeeping and chemical studies."[16] Gradually they became agrarian-industrialists as well; they borrowed money to establish mills and breweries on their estates—and no doubt would have wished to find in the old Prussia some of the underground wealth that the rich Silesian magnates found on their estates. The Junker was gradually distracted from his church-steeple perspective. He was drawn into the mainstream of economic life, concerned with the fluctuations of the market and with the rise of rival suppliers across the oceans, concerned with the impact of economic policy on his own well-being.

But however resourceful the Junkers may have been, other groups in society proved still more resourceful, and their rise could not but prove a challenge to Junker preeminence. Nor was it a material challenge alone. Under the impact of idealist thought, Prussia's civil society began to develop a new value, *Bildung*, a word that might be rendered inadequately as disciplined culture. Amidst the shambles of defeat, the University of Berlin was founded as the bastion of this new philosophical-historical learning. Other universities followed, and the *Bürger* had found a road to new distinction. Education became at once an end in itself—and as such it was exalted in society—and a means of social mobility—and as such it was suspect, particularly in aristocratic circles.[17] Out of the universities came vast numbers of a new elite—so vast in fact that there was distinct academic overpopulation in the 1830s and 1840s. The new elite could invoke its own universal ideal, the ideal of science and rationality, which it was expected would gradually weaken and destroy religious obscurantism and social mystification. In the early decades of the nineteenth century, German learning became justly renowned. In the cultural as well as the scientific disciplines, German universities helped to invent the method of invention. With success came pride and a quickened sense of political ambition. The academic class had a constitutional bias, even if the aged Bismarck's recollection that he left school a typical product of Prussian education with republican ideals was poetic exaggeration.

The Geman *Bürger* came to boast of *Besitz* as well as *Bildung*; property as well as culture were the values of civil society. After the post-Napoleonic slump, a new class of bankers and industrialists directed a great economic upswing. The railroad embodied the promise of the new era: it epitomized the successful harnessing of mechanical power; it symbolized the mobility of the new age; it required the concentration of unprecedented amounts of capital; and it opened up internal and external markets, proving a tremendous stimulus to the nation's economy. No wonder the industrialist Friedrich Harkort remarked in 1842 that "the nobility feels that the locomotive is the hearse in which feudalism will be carted off to the cemetery."[18] There was, to be sure, immense resistance in Germany to the railroads as well as to the new forms of capitalism.[19] But the "movers and doers," as Mack Walker in his impressive work called the new breed, throve despite sullen opposition. "Hometownsmen," again to use Walker's term, objected to the new breed much as did the old nobility: they thought of movers and doers as

> parts of the alien crowd that threatened to intrude upon them: disturbers, *Störer*, was a name the hometownsman applied to all of them, though he could not quite think of them collectively until a mobilized outside world seem collectivized against him. . . . Movers and doers were not rooted in the countryside. They emanated rather from the cities, and they could and did move regularly from one German city to another without serious change of personal habits or environments. The hometownsmen's place in the world depended on who he was in the community, and that was pretty much determined by the time he got citizenship rights; . . . the mover and doer was justified by what he did, a continuing process in which he confronted change and often sought it. Itinerant peddler, court lawyer, busy merchant, and the academically trained shared a social psychology hostile to that which underlay hometown life, and when

they came into contact with the home town they displayed it, each in his
own way.[20]

The new element, restless, dynamic, and successful, did threaten the
foundations of the old order, refurbished by the changes of the reform
era. The challenge to the aristocracy was implicit in the very phrase
"mobile wealth." To the Junker code, mobile wealth was a contradic-
tion in terms. Wealth was rooted in land—all other form of wealth
was suspect, morally and fiscally. Moreover, mobile wealth meant
steadily increasing fortunes—something that no Junker could hope to
emulate. In vain did Junkers deprecate the new spirit and the new
reality; in vain did they reassert their blue-blooded distinction, their
putative indifference to wealth. Merchants, bankers, and industrialists
made money and expected political influence; the Junkers objected
that the new way of life threatened traditional values, the corporate
spirit of the past, the happy deferential structure of society in which
every man knew his place. Marx understood their lament; he was the
first to see the magnitude of the change which the new forces represented:

> The bourgeoisie, wherever it has got the upper hand, has put an end to
> all feudal, patriarchal, idyllic relations. It has pitilessly torn asunder the
> motley feudal ties that bound man to his "natural superiors," and has
> left remaining no other nexus between man and man than naked self-
> interest, than callous "cash payment." It has drowned the most heavenly
> ectasies of religious fervor, of chivalrous enthusiasm, of Philistine senti-
> mentalism in the icy water of egotistical calculation. It has resolved
> personal worth into exchange value and, in place of the numberless in-
> defeasible chartered freedoms, has set up that single, unconscionable
> freedom—free trade. In one word, for exploitation, veiled by religious
> and political illusions, it has substituted naked, shameless, direct, brutal
> exploitation.
> The bourgeoisie has stripped of its halo every occupation hitherto
> honored and looked up to with reverent awe. It has converted the phy-
> sician, the lawyer, the priest, the poet, the man of science into its paid
> wage laborers.[21]

No wonder that decades later Theodor Fontane remarked in *Der
Stechlin* "that within all true Junkers there is a bit of Social Democracy."[22]

And yet Marx was only partially right. The Junkers survived the
corrosive power of capitalism and the revolutionary fervor of 1848.
They survived too and gradually subverted antinoble sentiment,
which was still strong in the early 1850s. In 1851, the social geographer
W. H. Riehl in his first major work asserted that the German *Bürger*

—or philistine as he sometimes called him—"will more easily return to a faith in the rationality of the devil incarnate than he will return to the faith in the rationality of the hereditary nobility." He noted also that the term "aristocracy" had become "a figure of speech . . . and people speak of money aristocracy, administration aristocracy, academic aristocracy." He added that "the aristocracy is the only one among the four great groups of society whose right to appear as a special estate [*Stand*] is denied by people who by no means are socialists. Nobody denies that there are *Bürger*, peasants, and proletarians, that this distinction is not accidental or arbitrary but rooted in conduct [*Sitte*] and vocation. . . . An aristocratic conduct may perhaps still exist—even if it is only misconduct—but an *aristocratic vocation* in our time has totally ceased to exist."[23] Riehl's summary of the antiaristocratic sentiment may have been exaggerated, though many writers and thinkers of the *Vormärz* echoed it, often in magnificent satire. The revolutions of 1848 were implicitly more antiaristocratic than antimonarchical; the *Paulskirche* debated whether to abolish the nobility not the monarchy.

In fact, the 1850s saw a great reversal of expectations. It was a decade of dynamic economic expansion and of political reaction. During it, the general condition of the nobility improved in every important aspect, and hence at the end of the century, the German sociologist Ferdinand Tönnies could write that "in the decade [1851–60] the Prussian nobility rose to its political flowering."[24] In that decade, under the intimidated and mystically inclined Frederick William IV, the Junkers increased their political power and social status, and their efforts at adaptability clearly paid off. Under the impact of events they had left their narrow circle.

In order to retain his privileged position in the civil administration, the Junker sent his younger sons to the university. Time and the Prussian reformers shook the Junkers out of their traditional insulation, out of the "rural idiocy," as Marx called it. By dint then of further adaptation—as well as by the quick favor bestowed on them by monarchs—the sons of the nobility once more flocked to the administration and the officer corps. (Let me here add parenthetically that these careers alleviated but did not solve the pecuniary problems of the nobility: the Prussian army and civil service were proud of their austerity. Salaries were low and demands for social respectability high; moreover, in the pre-1848 period and abundantly thereafter, the sons of the bourgeoisie often had greater resources at their command than the impoverished noble.) In the decades from 1820 to 1850, "the nobility succeeded in consolidating its leading position within the ad-

ministrative services."[25] In effect, this meant that over the years nobles outnumbered nonnobles at least in the higher echelons of the civil
service. Social composition had some bearing on the political outlook
as well; gradually the reform outlook of the bureaucracy faded. Some
nobles imbibed the ethos of Prussian officialdom and indeed often
were prouder of their calling than of their birth, but they retained
some attachment to the earlier order. Still, Bismarck complained bitterly about the liberal councillors who dominated his incompetent
ministerial colleagues in the early 1860s.

Despite the hopes and intentions of the reformers, the preponderance of nobles in the army became even more striking. Already in the
early 1840s the Junkers had a clear monopoly of the top positions. "In
1859 two thirds of all lieutenants, three quarters of the senior officers,
nine tenths of the generals were noblemen. Their actual influence in
the army was even greater, since the bourgeois element was largely
concentrated in the technical branches."[26]

In trying to understand the successful preservation of Junker power
in the first half of the century, one must remember that a key aspect
of Prussia's political culture was the effort of the state to blunt rather
than to accentuate the conflict between aspiring *Bürger* and old aristocracy. The government pursued policies that divided the *Bürgertum*: by means of extraordinary privileges in taxation and military
service, in marriage regulations, and in bureaucratic advancement, an
upper stratum of the *Bürgertum* became closely associated with the
state and separated from the great mass of the citizenry, who were
both underprivileged and deprived of their class leaders. In short, an
upper stratum of bureaucrats, academics, bankers, and merchants were
assimilated to privilege. In that sense, the aims of civil society and the
ideals of citizenship had been aborted. The pattern of intermarriage
reflected the new social order; upper *Bürgertum* and aristocracy inter-
married, while marrying below the privileged level remained a culpa-
ble affront to society. (It was a common experience in the nineteenth
century, often depicted in literature as well, that young officer or rich
Bürger would have to renounce his passionate inclination for a spouse
from the lower classes, often endowed with a natural humanity or a
simple goodness that had been bred out of the upper classes, dulled as
these were in correct, and often cold, bearing.[27]) The gap between
educated and uneducated, between the socially respectable and politically rewarded and the socially less respectable and politically unre-
warded, was allowed to grow while the distance between the nobility
and the privileged citizenry narrowed. To what extent this was the
result of conscious state action and to what extent it was an amalgam

of circumstances and motives is hard to say. The whole question of ascertainable consciousness in these processes—as against the retrospective diagnosis of motives by historians—is a problem to which I will want to return. One must also remember that commoners who bought noble estates and who assumed the same patrimonial rights that nobles exercised began to acquire noble values as well. Certainly the upper stratum of the *Bürgertum* practised what Hegel in one of his most ambiguous and most masterly phrases called "the heroism of flattery."[28] It was a sentiment that must be understood in its full complexity and must be seen as a pervasive, often unconscious, stance in the nineteenth century. It involved an act of self-abnegation, of patent insincerity, but it also described the possibility of bending not altogether unwillingly to something that was genuinely considered higher. It was a condition appropriate to rising classes that had left behind the formal deference of an earlier time but had not yet shaken the habits of nonage that had for so long been their custom.

The nobles' hold on the state had been preserved. The Reform Era had forced the Junkers to adjust to modern conditions of the market and to merit competition; once they had grasped what was involved they learned quickly, and their new position was the stronger for having been seemingly legitimized by the unaccustomed competition. The nobility also discovered that their traditional aura of distinction was an incalculable asset. The reforms, so to speak, had part-dragged, part-spurred them to success. As Reinhard Koselleck concludes, "The Reform era had different consequences in the political and in the social realm, put more concisely: in their long-range effect the reforms drove state and society apart."[29] This of course was the opposite of what the reformers intended.

Despite the rise of new elites, the Junkers had held their own in the first half of the century; in some ways, they had grown stronger by adaptation. The threats to their position remained, however, and in the early 1860s, at the time of Prussia's constitutional conflict, middle-class liberal exasperation with repressive privilege and with the whole anachronism of a feudal-militaristic caste broke forth again. A liberal political order would have altered the social order as well. In the end, the old order and its chief beneficiaries, the Junkers, were saved by an unsuspected Caesar in their midst, who for his own reasons was determined to save the monarchical system. Unpopular as it may be according to today's historiographical canons, it may still be argued

that Bismarck did play a decisive role in preserving the old social order
by creating a new political order. German unity—the dream of German liberals—was achieved by Bismarck's methods, and he thus successfully hitched nationalism to the old monarchical cause. In some
ways, Bismarck's work of 1862–71 approximated the work of the
earlier reformers: he too modernized Prussia sufficiently so that its
survival in a changed world was possible; and he too encountered the
most bitter objections from those elements—the old pietistic circles
among his fellow Junkers—that were closest to him and whose continued existence he assured. In the political sphere the liberals had been
defeated—and for decades after, many of them idolized their con-
queror.

The unaccustomed triumph of 1870 taught the *Bürger* new respect
for the Prussian state, for its rulers and its institutions. Extravagantly
staged victory parades brought home the triumph of the battlefield. In
the intoxication that followed the great reversal of fortune—for centuries, France had been the dominant military power of Europe—the
nobles as the embodiment of Prussian arms won new glory and prestige.

During the great economic boom of the 1850s and 1860s, which
reached its dizzying culmination with the speculative fever of the
early 1870s, the Junkers—or some of the more enterprising among
them—learned that prestige could be turned to profit—even as the
middle class began to learn that profit could be turned to prestige.
Junker indebtedness remained, and Friedrich Engels defined the problem pithily: "How to make it possible for the Old-Prussian country
Junkers to have an annual income of say 20,000 marks, an annual
expenditure of 30,000 marks and not to make any debts."[30] Some of
them solved this problem by becoming involved in the great industrial
promotions of the socalled *Gründerzeit*—as well-paid ornaments to
boards of directors that were often run by Jews.[31] The Junkers were
uneasy about their involvement in this modern world, but necessity
propelled them, and gradually *l'appetit vient en mangeant*.

These devices proved mere palliatives when the depression of the
1870s struck. In 1873 the stock market crash heralded the beginning
of the most protracted depression in modern German history. For the
Junkers, the most serious aspect of this crisis was the sudden importa-
tion of cheap grain from overseas—made possible by cheaper methods
of transportation—and the attendant decline in prices. (In the first
half of the 1880s the price of wheat in Germany dropped from an
average of 210 marks per ton to 162; other grains fared little better.[32])
The income of estate owners suffered, and the old Junker bugbear,

indebtedness and subsequent alienation, became more real still. By 1896 60 percent of the large estates in Prussia were mortgaged above 60 percent of their value. Even Bismarck, one of Prussia's largest landowners, complained about the meagre revenues from land. He was luckier than most: the bulk of his income came from timber and from various manufacturing enterprises that were run on his estates, and thus he was relatively immune to the vagaries of the grain market. Still, his banker Bleichröder had to warn him repeatedly not to indulge his unappeasable appetite for acquiring new land, at least not at the expense of investment in securities. The latter yielded 4 percent or better, which was higher than the yield on land.[33]

The Junkers fought back as best they could and with increasing desperation. In the late 1870s they abandoned free trade and won protective tariffs. In subsequent decades, they demanded ever higher rates, heedless of cost to the German consumer or to the deleterious effects of such tariffs on foreign policy, especially on Russo-German relations. Troubled by their absolute and relative decline—in the 1890s Germany finally became an industrial rather than an agrarian state, as measured by the indices of relative investment and population distribution—they importuned the state in any number of ways. They appeared in the political arena with formidable strength: their positions at court, in the government, and in the military afforded immense advantages; their hold on provincial and local administration, epitomized by their continued heavy presence as *Landräte* or country councillors, now proved vitally important.[34] Their own economic problems—Max Weber even spoke of the Junkers' death agony—coincided with the middle-class fear of the rising social democratic agitation. The agrarians had little difficulty in persuading their middle-class allies that the status quo was indivisible, that either all privileges would be protected or none would survive an imaginary revolution. If on a particular issue, the government—which intermittently had impulses of wishing to serve the public weal—or the Reichstag threatened to go counter to Junker wishes, the Junkers, now organized in the Conservative party, threatened all manner of revenge—including the repeated threat of the early 1890s that they would urge their followers to vote for Social Democrats. More and more the Junkers felt that time was against them.

They now reached out to demagogic politics. The Conservative party bolstered its nationalistic rhetoric with an undertone of anti-Semitism and appealed to large segments of the nonproletarian world with an ideology of strident illiberalism.[35] In 1893 the Junkers helped to organize the *Bund deutscher Landwirte*, which became their chief pressure group and which from the start adopted a strong anti-Semitic policy, beginning with the formal and explicit exclusion of Jews, despite the fact that many Jews had become estate owners.[36] Economic pressure forced them to rally their diffused power in state and society in order to survive. In the process, the exploiters of the nation appeared as its protectors, wrapped in a cloak of impeccable patriotism.

The Junkers could not, however, have succeeded by arrogance, avarice, and manipulation alone. The rest of society was not simply coerced; other strata of society retained a willing subordination to the Junkers, a lingering deference to their values.

It has become almost an historical cliche to say that the amalgam of business, academic, administrative, and noble elites agreed on common economic policies and on a common political strategy not to allow the lower classes to augment their political position in any manner. I believe this common front to have existed; I will return to it later. Here let me make but one cautionary point: in stressing this common front against the lower classes, in ascribing its bent for imperialism and its rhetoric of social imperialism—are we not sometimes in danger of imposing our consciousness on the consciousness of people in the past? What concerns me in the recent orthodoxies of German historiography is a relative disregard for what people of the time felt and thought. We have learned that what people say may not be what they mean, but we cannot assume that they mean what they do not say. The conflicts within the elites, even between Junkers and *Grossbürgertum*, were often muted, but they should not be neglected. Obviously a clue to people's thoughts and sentiments can be found in their unstated values, in the habits of their lives, in the models that they choose.

If we look at German culture from 1870 to 1914, we see in familiar detail the hegemony that earlier modes of life and earlier values exercised over the new elites. We note the imitation of the landed elite in the wholesale buying of landed estates by the rising class of plutocrats; Bismarck's banker Bleichröder, for example, bought Field Marshal Roon's estate. Once on these estates, they hoped to emulate the style of their bankrupt superiors. We see rich entrepreneurs having their portraits painted and their family tree refurbished; we see a common yearning for distinctions, for orders, titles, and for the ultimate in psychic luxury, ennoblement. Among the rich, but also among the academic and administrative elites, we see the furtive glance upwards, not the patrician look of satisfaction. But beyond this social unease— so clear also in the pattern of intermarriage—is the permeation of society with specifically nonbourgeois habits and values: one thinks of the student fraternity with the enforced heroism of duelling, the status of the reserve officer in civilian society, the prestige of the uniform. This idolatry of *Schneidigkeit*, brainless virility mixed with punctilious brutality, was often caricatured at the time. All of this was sanctified by the aristocratic nature of the imperial court and the authoritarian, conservative stance of the Protestant Church.[37]

The diffusion of the noncivilian spirit reached its height at a time when the landed nobility faced its gravest economic crisis. But did this diffusion not contain something more than the frightened and repressed conduct of a frightened and repressive amalgam of elites? I think it can also be seen in another perspective—admittedly one more nebulous and perhaps less important than the more conventional ones. This deference to Junker values is the product no doubt of military triumphs and political anxieties, but in the last analysis one must wonder whether it did not also represent a kind of voluntary subordination before a more persistent ideal. Some nobles had long since become cost-conscious agronomists and greed-stricken speculators in stocks and bonds, but they were honored for their continued pose as being a precapitalistic class. They had appeal precisely because they seemed to combine personal freedom with a relatively strict moral code—which, in principle and not infrequently in practice, they obeyed to the point of death. They were thought of as men of honor and of service, correct and incorruptible. One admired their moral certainty, their often impoverished but proud existence; one admired those cold, steely eyes that did not cast an envious look upward. One admired them for their uncomplaining endurance, their *"aushalten,"* as it was called.[38] One admired them as well for their seeming disregard for money. Money was not an end for them but a means; they felt as Heine felt who candidly avowed, "Money is my Freedom." Their affectation of poverty was much more appealing than the ostentatious display of opulence, the dazzling tastelessness of the plutocrats. More: one sensed and often envied their rootedness in land, their proximity to nature, their familiarity with life as it had been lived for millenia, dependent on the exigencies of climate and crop. The Junkers were communitarian, averse to the bourgeois work ethic although obedient to their own demands of duty, and they were on easy terms with common folk. They knew their peasants and loved their animals; they were—or so it seemed to the envious outsider—unbrokenly themselves, less affected, less afraid. For all their speculations and political machinations, for all their meanness and deceit, something of an old and purer world clung to them. They embodied, in short, something of the dream of the antibourgeois which was so powerful in Europe throughout the nineteenth century. The Junker combined a host of traits—and in the stuffy materialistic world of the 1870s appeared as a kind of noble hippy.

The Junkers relied on their own relentless pressure and on the sway of their ideal, made visible by their unique role in Germany's most cherished possession, the army. At the very time of their economic decline, they could still impose their values on classes that were in the ascendancy. This shift in values—more apparent perhaps than real—has led some historians to speak of the refeudalization of Germany; perhaps it would be more accurate to say that certain remnants of a Prussian feudal hegemony had never been dismantled. But by focusing on social developments, it has become easier, I believe, than it used to be to see the continuity of German history in the nineteenth century, without once again succumbing to the old fatality of seeing it as a process of inevitable development, as the Prussian school of historians has done and as the Western historians who interpret Nazism as the logical outcome of German history have also done.

From the late 1870s on, the Junkers clung to power and exploited their prestige in order to persuade the nation—or the part of it that mattered—that the economic survival of Junkers was a most urgent and proper concern for the nation itself. If Junkerdom were allowed to perish, if its economic base were allowed to erode, if Germany were no longer to have Junker grain or Junker officers in case of war, then the nation itself would perish. Some critics at the time saw that behind Junker nationalism hid Junker selfishness and that behind Junker practice hid an appalling disregard for the national good, but for the respectable part of German society, Junker selfishness and hypocrisy became one more national taboo, an unacknowledged burden.

The more the Junkers claimed to be the sole protectors of the nation's honor and wartime food supply, the more they pursued policies that injured the nation. In the mid-1880s even so conservative a man as Johannes von Miquel thought that the depopulation of the land in the east had gone so far that a modest scheme of "internal colonization" would be necessary in order to shore up and alleviate conditions in Elbia. He proposed a scheme of transferring—with compensation of course—between one-seventh and one-eighth of the land held in large estates to independent peasants. The conservative outcry sufficed to kill the proposal.[39]

It was Max Weber in his 1895 Inaugural Lecture who with scholarly precision and political passion laid bare the true consequences of Junker policies in East Elbia. He pointed to the growing replacement of valuable German by inferior Polish workers, thus decreasing the German and increasing the alien element in an historic and exposed province. Half a million German laborers had left the east in less than a decade; as Weber said, "in the dull, half-conscious drive to go away lies a measure of primitive idealism: whoever cannot fathom it, does not know the magic of freedom."[40] The landowners of East Elbia knew neither the magic of freedom nor the imperatives of national policy. In the perspective of the day, to augment the Polish element in the exposed frontier regions of the Reich was a precarious undertaking. In the same lecture, Weber, himself a patriot and even an imperialist, warned against allowing an economically declining class to exercise preeminent political power. He concluded, however, that neither of the two other classes were equipped to wield power. His Inaugural Lecture was a kind of unwilling epitaph for the political system of the Second Empire.

Max Weber was not the only conservative who was worried over the hollowness of Junker rule. Throughout his life, Theodor Fontane dwelt lovingly, if ironically, on the foibles of East Elbian aristocracy. In perhaps his greatest work, *Effi Briest*, completed in 1893, he suggests something of the tension between an anachronistic Junker code and the claims of life. When, in the novel, von Instetten discovers that his wife has some years before had an adulterous affair, he decides to fight a duel with her former lover (whom he subsequently kills). His best friend laments the contemplated duel and says: "Our cult of honor is idol-worship, but we must subordinate ourselves to it as long as the idol reigns." (In the same novel, at an earlier point, the wife's father remarks about his only granddaughter: "If things go on like this, then Annie will in due time have to marry a banker [hopefully a Christian banker, if such will still exist]"; and he hopes the king will allow their offspring to carry an aristocratic name.) In his correspondence, Fontane went much further; in 1896 he wrote, not without pathos, that his "unhappy love affair" with the Prussian nobility was over. It had turned to distaste: "The stance of the nobility—almost going beyond the purely political—has taken on a shameless character, not externally, but internally . . . a horrible mixture of narrowness, arrogance, and selfishness fills the whole brood."[41] This internal decay of a class that, as even Treitschke put it, "regarded a career in the stable as more honorable than a career in science"[42] aroused growing concern. Werner Sombart and Robert Michels, for example, noted the terrible degeneration in the level of culture and education of the Prussian nobility, who were more insulated from the intellectual life of the nation than ever before.[43] And all of these misgivings were publicly and effectively voiced in the humor magazines of the time, especially in the newer and more daring journal, *Simplicissimus*. The ignorant, arrogant, brutal Junker was elevated to a stereotype in the pages of these magazines—and life insisted on imitating art, as the Zabern affair of 1912 made abundantly clear.[44]

The disenchantment with the Junker regime coincided then with the maximum degree of noble pressure and middle-class anxiety. In the years before the Great War, the fact that Germany had but one upper stratum, so inextricably linked in its parts as to make the reform of any one of them virtually impossible, became more and more apparent. In 1914 Michels wrote: "In today's Germany . . . there is no socially independent bourgeoisie with pride in itself. In its upper reaches the German bourgeoisie is only a threshold [*Vorstufe*] to the nobility." It sought to be accepted by the nobility in order to be dissolved in it.[45] Successive chancellors—most notably Bethmann Hollweg—condemned in private the anxious *immobilisme*, the wilful irresponsibility, of this amalgam which in public they had to labor to defend. In private, Bethmann confided: "To change East Elbia is an impossibility; [it] must be broken . . . disappear."[46] Middle-class chauvinism and Junker arrogance robbed Germany of whatever chances it had for even a modicum of political sanity in the conduct of the war.

The Junkers had fought a triumphant battle against their own decline. As Ralf Dahrendorf put it: "The power elite of Imperial Germany was monopolistic in that its ancient core of Prussian Junker and officials clearly set the tone by which all others tuned their instruments. . . . The elite of Junker and civil servants maintained its power long enough to shape not only German politics of the time but German society of the following epochs as well. The success of its unchecked self-interest—for this it was, although in the end the "common good" was involved probably by habit rather than malice—proved a Pyrrhic victory, whose astronomical cost has to be paid by German society."[47] The cost was indeed staggering and included the disastrous ineptitude of Germany's diplomacy before the First World War, the fatality of her wartime policies, the frenzied failure of Weimar, and her self-destruction under Hitler. In each phase, the Junkers in their corporate actions—despite the many acts of individual bravery—betrayed German society and undermined the possibilities of some half-way stopping place to total disaster. In the months before their final demise, the Junker class—or leading representatives of it—snatched a moment of heroic greatness in which to disappear from history. The men who sought to overthrow Hitler on 20 July 1944 were to a large extent scions of the oldest East Prussian nobility; in the last months of his reign, Hitler finally unleashed his full hatred of that class, as conspirator after conspirator was hanged from the gallows. What Hitler began—the liquidation of a class that had played so monumental and so ambiguous a role in Prussian-German history—Stalin completed. The manor houses of the Junker were burned by the advancing Soviet armies and their land expropriated by the Soviet puppets in East Germany. The landed elite of East Elbia ceased to exist—its good interred even before its death.

NOTES

1. The classical analysis of this is Thorstein Veblen, *Imperial Germany and the Industrial Revolution* (New York, 1942). One of the best recent treatments of the theme is Ralf Dahrendorf, *Society and Democracy in Germany* (Garden City, N.Y., 1967).

2. Alexander Gerschenkron, *Bread and Democracy in Germany*, rev. ed. (New York, 1966), p. vii.

3. Theodore Zeldin, *France, 1848–1945* (Oxford, 1973), p. 19.

4. F. L. Carsten, *The Origins of Prussia* (Oxford, 1954), p. 272; for the rise of the Junkers see part 2.

5. John R. Gillis, "Aristocracy and Bureaucracy in Nineteenth-Century Prussia," *Past and Present* 40 (1968): 103–29.

6. On the other hand, the Legal Code breathed premature modernity. Thus it formally decreed: "Every healthy mother is obligated to nurse her own infants." Klaus Epstein, *The Genesis of German Conservatism* (Princeton, 1966), p. 378.

7. Hajo Holborn, *A History of Modern Germany, 1648–1840* (New York, 1964), p. 353.

8. Gillis, "Aristocracy and Bureaucracy," p. 109. See also Walter M. Simon, *The Failure of the Prussian Reform Movement, 1807–1819* (Ithaca, N.Y., 1955).

9. Walter Görlitz, *Die Junker* (Glücksburg, 1956), p. 195.

10. Hans Rosenberg, *Bureaucracy, Aristocracy, and Autocracy: The Prussian Experience, 1660–1815* (Cambridge, Mass., 1958), p. 220; Reinhart Koselleck, *Preussen zwischen Reform und Revolution: Allgemeines Landrecht, Verwaltung und soziale Bewegung von 1791 bis 1848*, 2nd ed. (Stuttgart, 1975), p. 83.

11. Michael G. Mulhall, *The Dictionary of Statistics* (London, 1889), p. 483.

12. Theodore S. Hamerow, *Restoration, Revolution, Reaction: Economics and Politics in Germany, 1815–1871* (Princeton, 1958), p. 226. See also Hans-Ulrich Wehler, *Das deutsche Kaiserreich, 1871–1918* (Göttingen, 1973), pp. 20–24; Holborn, *Germany, 1648–1840*, pp. 409, 465.

13. Hans-Jürgen Puhle, *Politische Agrarbewegungen in kapitalistischen Industriegesellschaften: Deutschland, U.S.A., und Frankreich im 20. Jahrhundert* (Göttingen, 1975), p. 44.

14. Koselleck, *Preussen zwischen Reform und Revolution*, p. 516.

15. *From Max Weber: Essays in Sociology*, trans. and ed. H. H. Gerth and C. Wright Mills (New York, 1958), pp. 367, 382–83.

16. Otto von Bismarck, *Die gesammelten Werke* (Berlin, 1933), 14: 58.

17. The hostility of some elements in society to the modern ideals of education

can be gleaned from a tract that the Badenese official J. G. Schlosser wrote in 1776 (it is not altogether illicit to suggest that the antiquated notions of a Badenese official of 1776 approximated the latest ideas of an embattled Junker in 1811): "The vocations of men are in most cases so incompatible with the all around development of their faculties that I would almost say that one cannot start early enough to encourage the atrophy of two-thirds of those faculties; for most men are destined for vocations where they cannot use them in later life. Why do you castrate oxen and colts when you prepare them for the yoke and cart, yet wish to develop the totality of human powers in men similarly condemned to the yoke and the cart? They will jump the furrow if you give them the wrong preparation, or kick against the traces until they die." Quoted in Epstein, *The Genesis of German Conservatism*, p. 79.

18. Quoted in Dietrich Eichholtz, *Junker und Bourgeoisie vor 1848 in der preussischen Eisenbahngeschichte* (East Berlin, 1962), p. 37.

19. See Franz Schnabel, *Deutsche Geschichte im Neunzehnten Jahrhundert*, 2nd ed. (Freiburg, 1950), 3: 371–393; Manfred Riedel, "Vom Biedermeier zum Maschinenzeitalter: Zur Kulturgeschichte der ersten Eisenbahnen in Deutschland," *Archiv für Kulturgeschichte* 43 (1961): 100–123.

20. Mack Walker, *German Home Towns: Community, State, and General Estate, 1648–1871* (Ithaca and London, 1971), pp. 119–20.

21. Karl Marx and Friedrich Engels, *The Communist Manifesto*, reprinted in Lewis Feuer, ed., *Basic Writings on Politics and Philosophy* (Garden City, N.Y., 1959), pp. 9–10.

22. Theodor Fontane, *Der Stechlin* (Berlin, 1898), p. 270.

23. W. H. Riehl, *Die bürgerliche Gesellschaft* (Stuttgart and Tübingen, 1851), pp. 116–19.

24. Ferdinand Tönnies, "Deutscher Adel im 19. Jahrhundert," *Neue Rundschau* 2 (1912): 1057.

25. Koselleck, *Preussen zwischen Reform und Revolution*, p. 434.

26. Hajo Holborn, *A History of Modern Germany, 1840–1945* (New York, 1969), p. 137; Koselleck, *Preussen zwischen Reform und Revolution*, p. 435.

27. Koselleck, *Preussen zwischen Reform und Revolution*, p. 107.

28. See Lionel Trilling, *Sincerity and Authenticity* (Cambridge, Mass., 1972), pp. 34–36.

29. Koselleck, *Preussen zwischen Reform und Revolution*, p. 437.

30. Quoted in Gerschenkron, *Bread and Democracy in Germany*, p. 46.

31. See my "Money, Morals, and the Pillars of Society," in *The Failure of Illiberalism: Essays on the Political Culture of Modern Germany* (New York, 1972); and chap. 10 of my *Gold and Iron*, (New York, 1977).

32. Kenneth D. Barkin, *The Controversy over German Industrialization, 1890–1902* (Chicago and London, 1970), p. 27.

33. Puhle, *Politische Agrarbewegungen*, pp. 44–45; also Hans Rosenberg, "Die 'Demokratisierung' der Rittergutsbesitzerklasse," *zur Geschichte und Problematik der Demokratie*, Festgabe für Hans Herzfeld (Berlin, 1958). For details of Bismarck's private fortune see my *Gold and Iron*, chaps. 5 and 12.

34. See Lysbeth W. Muncy, "The Prussian Landräte in the Years of the Monarchy: A Case Study of Pomerania and the Rhineland in 1890–1918," *Central European History* 6, no. 4 (December, 1973): 299–338, as well as her earlier *The Junker in the Prussian Administration under William II, 1888–1914* (Providence, R.I., 1944).

35. The political use of anti-Semitism should not lead one to suppose that Junkers were particularly given to anti-Semitic views or positions. To the contrary. The relations between Junker and Jew were functional and often even harmonious, and generally the Junker tended to be aloof from vulgar or extreme prejudice and certainly from racial anti-Semitism.

36. See Wehler, *Kaiserreich*, p. 48; Barkin, *The Controversy*, pp. 60–67; also

Hans-Jürgen Puhle, *Agrarische Interessenpolitik und preussischer Konservatismus in wilhelminischen Reich, 1893–1914* (Hanover, 1966).

37. The best caricature of this aspect of German society is still Heinrich Mann's *Der Untertan*. We find echoes of it in the novels of Theodor Fontane and in Hermann Broch's *The Sleepwalkers*. Among historians, Eckart Kehr was one of the first to point to the pernicious sway of Junker customs and others have followed in his footsteps. However, a full historical treatment of the Junkers remains to be done—and when it is done, it must also record their virtues and their ideals, subjects that are harder to depict than their power and their will to power. At their best, they tried to live up to their own demanding ideals and they were hard on their own transgressions. Like so much else in German history, they have perhaps been seen too much from the perspective of 1945. A full portrait would also have to take account of the perceptions of Junkerdom abroad; it would have to mention the depiction of ambiguous and anachronistic Junker virtues in Jean Renoir's classic film of the 1930s *La Grande Illusion*. Some evocation of declining Junker life can be found in Joachim von Dissow, *Adel im Ubergang: Ein kritischer Standesgenosse berichtet aus Residenzen und Gutshäusern* (Stuttgart, 1961).

38. They certainly meant to be exemplars of that old Prussian adage: learn how to suffer without complaining. It was left to one of their critics, hardly a disinterested one, Eugen Richter, leader of the Progressives, to invert this injunction and to assert that in light of Junker economic pressure it seemed that the Junkers had learned to complain without suffering. Richter changed *Lerne zu leiden ohne zu klagen* to *Lerne zu klagen ohne zu leiden*. Quoted in Puhle, *Politische Agrarbewegungen*, p. 51.

39. Hans Herzfeld, *Johannes von Miquel* (Detmold, 1938), 2: 84ff.

40. Max Weber, *Gesammelte Politische Schriften* (Munich, 1921), pp. 12–13.

41. Theodor Fontane, *Briefe an Georg Friedlaender*, ed. Kurt Schreinert (Heidelberg, 1954), pp. 300–301.

42. Quoted in Tönnies, "Deutscher Adel," p. 1062.

43. Robert Michels, *Probleme der Sozialphilosophie* (Leipzig and Berlin, 1914), p. 143.

44. Ann Jobling, "'A Playful Judgment,' Satire and Society in Wilhelmine Germany" (Ph.D. diss., Columbia Univ., 1974).

45. Michels, *Probleme*, p. 151.

46. Quoted in my *The Failure of Illiberalism*, p. 109.

47. Dahrendorf, *Society and Democracy*, pp. 223, 224.

4 | Russia*

The Russian nobility differed in its origins and in its role from the nobility of the other lands of Europe. Unlike its peers in those lands the nobility of Russia owed its preeminence to the civil and military functions that it performed in the service of the tsar, and not to the ownership of land. Elevation into the nobility did not necessarily include a grant of land; indeed, as time went by an ever larger number of the nobility was landless or nearly so. The Russian nobility was thus not a territorial elite, nor was it the heir of a feudal nobility. Russia had no feudal castles. In days long gone rival princes and their followers had possessed regional power bases. The princes of Moscow, however, in their savage ascent to absolute authority, had destroyed all vestiges of regional autonomy and wiped out most of the men who once possessed it. The continued expansion of the Muscovite hegemony, the tsars' practice of resettling nobles as their realm grew, and the long absence of nobles on the tsar's service aborted the growth of new roots into the land and of ancestral claims to the loyalties of the local people. Even the surnames of Russian nobles revealed the absence of local associations. Unlike the nobles of western Europe they did not take their names from places; in Russia, as Maurice Baring remarked, there was no von und zu, no de, no Lord So-and-So of So-and-So[1].

Until well into the eighteenth century the Russian nobility did not even have a collective name. The one finally settled upon was *dvorianstvo*. The choice of that word was significant. *Dvorianstvo* does not mean nobility, a word that comes from the latin *nobilis* and means renowned or outstanding. *Dvorianstvo* means the people of the ruler's court, his *dvor*. It was an old term. It had been used centuries before

I am indebted to Dr. Robert V. Allen of the Library of Congress and to Dr. S. Frederick Starr of the Kennan Institute for Russian Studies for their advice and assistance in the preparation of this essay.

for the men who actually lived at court, the ruler's retinue and his menials. In the sixteenth and seventeenth centuries it had meant those who held land in return for service to the ruler and who ranked between the *boiars*, the great lords, and the *deti boiarskie*, the lesser servitors. Now all nobles, great and small, were called the *dvorianstvo*, the men of the court. It was a fitting name for an elite who owed its status to the services it gave to the ruler.

The Russian nobility differed, too, from its European counterparts in the matter of titles. Very few Russian nobles had hereditary titles. *Kniaz*, prince, was the sole native hereditary title. Until the eighteenth century only descendants of the princes of medieval Russia could claim it. Later the tsars bestowed the rank and title on favorites, albeit sparingly. Starting in the eighteenth century, too, the tsars gave the title of count or baron to others to whom they wished to show special favor.[2]

Despite their rarity (or perhaps because of it) titles did not possess the lustre that attached to them in western Europe. Some of the greatest families had no titles and apparently felt no need to get them. Nor did the possession of a title guarantee status and prestige. All children bore the title of their parents even while their parents lived. Moreover, in the course of a few generations partible inheritance, by which property was divided among all male heirs, coupled with the prodigality so common among Russian nobles, reduced branches of many titled families to poverty and obscurity. Long before the fabled 1920s when, if the breathless accounts of tourists and of Hollywood movies are to be believed, nearly every other gigolo, waiter, or cabdriver in Paris was a Russian aristocrat, bearers of splendid titles earned their livings at home and abroad as musicians in cafe orchestras, as cabdrivers and maids, and in other modest pursuits.[3]

Instead of a territorial base or an ancestral claim, nobility (except for a few families of ancient pedigree) depended upon rank achieved in the service of the tsar. In 1722 Peter I had established a Table of Ranks of fourteen grades (*chin*) in both the civil and military services. Men of nonnoble origin acquired hereditary nobility when they entered the lowest (fourteenth) grade in the military or when they reached the eighth grade in the civil service. Up to the end of tsarist Russia in 1917 every noble either held an ennobling *chin* in the Table of Ranks or was a descendant of a man who had done so.

By this institutionalization of elevation into the nobility, Peter established the supremacy of service to the tsar over noble birth. From then on, to be a noble meant to be a servitor of the tsar or a descendant of a servitor. Until 1762 every noble had to serve in the military or the bureaucracy in order to retain his nobility. Then Peter III abolished compulsory service and allowed each noble to decide for himself whether he wished to serve. The introduction of the Table of Ranks had the effect, too, of making the Russian nobility open-ended by its automatic elevation of men of plebian origin into the nobility when they reached the designated grade. This openness kept the nobility from becoming a self-contained caste that could draw up its own rules for entry. The nobility was rudely reminded of this late in the nineteenth century when it tried to determine admission into its ranks. Alexander III's powerful minister of internal affairs, Count Dmitrii Tolstoi, pointed out to the tsar that "the Russian *dvorianstvo* is not of feudal oirgin and as a service estate it cannot have the right of self-determination without changing its historical significance."[4]

There were other avenues into the nobility, but these never became principal ones. The tsar at his pleasure could grant a patent of hereditary nobility. The award of certain decorations for valor or distinguished service carried nobility with it. There was also a rank called personal nobility accorded to those who reached the grade in the Table of Ranks immediately beneath the one that gave hereditary nobility. The personal noble enjoyed most of the privileges of the hereditary noble, save that personal nobility extended only to himself and his spouse but not to his heirs.[5]

Peter I had intended that every servitor, no matter how distinguished his origins, should begin his career at the lowest grade and that promotion should depend upon merit and length of service. Those intentions quickly foundered on the realities of influence and connections. Hereditary nobles gained preferential treatment in promotions and in appointment to high office. Men with higher education—and until well into the second half of the nineteenth century higher education was a near-monopoly of the nobility—were exempted from passing through the lower grades. And, of course, the Autocrat of All the Russias could disregard his own law and make direct appointments to any grade.

The names of the grades in the Table of Ranks of the civil service were mainly transliterations or translations of German offices. The highest grade was *kantsler*, chancellor; next came *deistvitel'nyi tainyi sovetnik*, the Russian translation of *wirkliche Geheimrat*; then *tainyi sovetnik*, or *Geheimrat*; and so on down the list. These names give little indication of the duties of the grades. Each grade had its own uniform, and the garniture of uniforms increased in direct proportion to increases in rank. Each grade, too, had its prescribed form of address. The men in the lowest grade were addressed as "well born," those in the next as "high well born," those in the next as "high born," and so on up the ladder of superlatives to "Excellency" and "High Excellency."

Territorial expansion, increase in population, further involvement in European power politics, a huge increase in the military establishment, and the entrance of the state into new sectors of activity provided an always growing need for civil and military servitors. That meant more people in the nobility as men rose in the expanded bureaucracy and the armed forces. Natural increase helped account for the growth, too, since all direct descendants of an hereditary noble were themselves noble. The abolition in 1762 of the service requirement also contributed to the increase in numbers. Many nobles continued to serve, but others did not enter service or else remained in service for a short period and then retired. Moreover, by and large, nobles preferred the more glamorous military to the civil service. These circumstances compelled the government to recruit many of its higher civil officials from other orders of society. Thus some were the sons of "honorary citizens" (a privileged estate created by imperial decree in 1832 and composed of upper bourgeoisie); others were the sons of merchants and the petty bourgeoisie; and still others—a large group—were the sons of priests. Between 1825 and 1845 some 20,000 men of nonnoble origin, and between 1875 and 1896 some 30,000, achieved hereditary nobility through promotion in the Table of Ranks.[6]

These numbers seem large until they are compared with Russia's total population and with the ratio of nobles to population in some other lands. In 1858 there were 609,973 hereditary nobles of both sexes in the fifty provinces (*gubernii*) of European Russia. That was about 1 percent of the population. A disproportionate number of nobles, however, lived in the nine Baltic, White Russian, and Lithuanian provinces. If these provinces with their swarms of Polish and German nobles are left out of account the number of nobles in the forty-one provinces of Great Russia and the Ukraine was 232,346. That was about .45 percent of the population. By 1897 the number of nobles in the fifty provinces of European Russia had risen by 45 percent to 885,754. But total population had experienced an even more spectacular rise, so that the ratio of nobles to the total population had fallen to .95 percent. In the forty-one Great Russian and Ukrainian provinces the number of nobles had more than doubled to 477,836. That amounted to slightly more than one-half of 1 percent of the population. The number of personal nobles rose sharply, too. In 1858 there were 276,809 of them in the fifty provinces and 251,205 in the forty-one Great Russian and Ukrainian provinces. In 1897 these numbers had mounted to 486,963 and 432,664 respectively.[7]

Peter I's creation of the Table of Ranks was part of his plan to

restructure Russian society. He began the process of enrolling each of
his subjects into a legally established estate or order (*soslovie*). The
four major estates were nobles, clergy, townsmen, and peasants. As
time passed these basic estates were subdivided and some of the subdi-
visions became independent orders. Each order had its own legally
defined rights and obligations. There was also a category, called the
inorodtsy, that stood outside the hierarchy of orders and had its own
special—and inferior—legal status. This order included the native
tribesmen of the frontier regions and the Jews. By the second half of
the nineteenth century every subject of the tsar belonged to an order,
identified himself as a member of his order, and had the privileges and
obligations that were peculiar to it.[8]

By creating orders and by making the acquisition of nobility dependent upon service to the throne Peter welded the nobility into a
corporate body. In the lands of western Europe a centuries-old struggle against the encroachments of the throne had evoked and sustained
a corporate spirit in the nobility. In Russia the corps of the nobility
was the creation of the throne: as MacKenzie Wallace put it, the
nobility was "crushed into a conglomerate by the weight of the autocratic power."[9] The transformation into a privileged corporate
order was completed when Catherine II issued the Charter of the
Nobility in 1785. It codified the privileges the nobility already possessed and gave it new powers in local and provincial government.

An awareness of their special status as a privileged order and of their
common interests quickly manifested itself among Russian nobles.
Men whose fathers and grandfathers had humbly referred to themselves as servants (*kholopy*) of the tsar, and who until 1762 could be
whipped like common peasants when they displeased him, now spoke
of themselves as "the corps of the nobility which includes within itself
its own prerogatives and invulnerability."[10] Already in the middle of
the eighteenth century spokesmen of the nobility urged that entry
into its ranks through promotion in the services be abolished or at least
restricted, claiming that new men lacked the qualities of mind and
character that hereditary nobles possessed. In response to repeated
demands of this sort the sovereigns periodically raised the threshold
for admission into the hereditary nobility, until in 1856 it was set at
the fourth grade of the civil service and the sixth grade (colonel or
naval captain) in the military service. That still did not satisfy the
nobility, which persisted in its agitation for still more exclusivity, but
without further success.[11]

The phenomenon of corporate solidarity did not diminish the
autocratic power and authority of the tsar. The tradition of loyalty

and obedience to the sovereign weakened hardly at all. The nobles of Russia did not demand that their ruler share part of his authority with them, except during those strange decades after the death of Peter I when nobles made and unmade tsars and tsaritsas. They owed their status and their privileges and even their existence as a corporate body to the sovereign and they saw no reason to oppose his prerogatives. Even though the service requirement was abolished in 1762 nobles continued to serve, for up to the end of the tsarist regime the road to high position and prestige and power still started and ended at the steps of the throne. The tsars for their part were so confident of the loyalty of the nobility that they ordered revolutionary changes, such as Alexander II's emancipation of the serfs, with little or no consideration for the interests of the nobility. The nobles might protest, but they always went along.

This acquiescence of the nobility weakened its corporate solidarity and its influence. For example, the Charter of the Nobility of 1785 had ordered the hereditary nobility of each county and province to organize itself into an assembly and had given these assemblies control over much of the local administration. The government, however, soon made it clear that it intended to maintain firm control over these assemblies and that it viewed independent expression or action by an assembly as resistance to the will of the tsar. Even more important, the governor of the province, appointed by the tsar and answerable only to him, had nearly unlimited authority. Small wonder that most nobles showed scant interest in these assemblies and that sparse attendance marked the required meetings. In 1836 the government tried to lend new prestige to the assemblies by raising the property qualifications for voting at the meetings, hoping to make the assemblies more exclusive and therefore more attractive. It also ordered fines of 25 to 250 rubles for missing the meetings. After the emancipation in 1861 the government tried the opposite tack and sharply reduced the property qualifications, except for nobles who owned urban property. These efforts to stimulate interest met with failure. Save for a rare outburst of action or protest by an individual assembly, the required triennial meetings were little more than social occasions to renew old acquaintances.[12]

There were times when nobles had briefly abandoned their traditional subservience. They had overthrown and slain tsars in palace revolutions. In the Decembrist revolt of 1825 they sought to end the tsar's absolute power. They participated in and even led movements, liberal, radical, and revolutionary, that kept imperial Russia in turmoil during the last decades of its existence. Nor was the relationship between crown and nobility strained by nobles alone. The strange and unpredictable Paul III (1796–1801) followed an antinoble policy during his brief reign, cancelling many noble privileges. But Paul could not turn back the clock. He was brutally murdered by disaffected nobles, and his son and successor, Alexander I, as one of the first acts of his reign, restored the privileges that Paul had taken away. These disturbances of the relationship between tsar and nobility were only episodic. Each needed the other too much to risk permanent alienation. The dependence of the nobility upon the throne for status and privilege had its counterweight in the dependence of the throne upon the nobility. Nobles provided the core of the civil and military services, and the tsar depended upon them to maintain and defend the established order in which throne and nobility were the two dominating forces.

The privileges allowed the nobility by the throne extended to all nobles so that legally they were all equally noble and equally privileged. The legal fiction did not conceal the real situation. There were accepted gradations in privilege, power, and social standing. There were registers, called Books of the Nobility, that separated the nobility into six descending social categories.[13] Stratification was more pronounced and meaningful when the ownership of property was used as the standard. Until the emancipation in 1861 real property was measured not in terms of acreage but in terms of adult male serfs, called "souls." In 1858, 43 percent of the 103,880 serfowners had fewer than 21 souls each. Another 34 percent had 21 to 100 souls, 19 percent had 101 to 500 souls, and 3 percent owned more than 500 souls each. Collectively, the 43 percent who owned fewer than 21 souls owned only 3 percent of the 10½ million serf souls, while the 3 percent who had over 500 souls owned 44 percent of all serf souls.[14] Clearly most serf owners were men of limited or at best modest means. Many had difficulties in making ends meet. In 1858 the marshall of the nobility of the fertile agricultural province of Riazan reported that 1,700 noble families, or one-fourth of all the noble families of that province, were so poor that "together with their peasants they form one family, eat at one table and live in one hut."[15] Still other nobles owned neither land nor serfs. Mostly bureaucrats and army officers, they depended upon their salaries for their principal or only source of income. These landless nobles first appeared in the eighteenth century and their numbers grew steadily as the decades went by.

The topmost stratum of the nobility, made up of a relatively small group of families, was known collectively as the *znat'*, the notables. They clustered in St. Petersburg and in Moscow. Though they included families of old pedigree, high official rank and at least a patina of general culture provided the real basis for membership. To insulate themselves against the flood of new nobles and to keep the parvenus and the bumpkins at a distance, the notables used the device of language. Their children were taught from early youth to speak Parisian French without accent and with elegance of vocabulary. That became the language of high society. During the French Revolution émigrés who sought sanctuary in Russia brought with them the fashions and ideas of the *ancien régime*. They became teachers in schools that restricted their enrollment to sons of the great families and that indoctrinated them in the social graces and the values of old France. Lesser families attempted to ape their betters, so that the supply of qualified teachers soon must have fallen far behind demand. Doubtless many noble households had tutors as inept as the one-time barber and soldier who was hired to teach young Grinev in Pushkin's tale of *The Captain's Daughter*, whose only qualification was that he happened to be a Frenchman.

The greatest families lived for part of the year in their town houses and palaces in St. Petersburg and Moscow. The men who spent their careers in government service lived there too, and in provincial capitals as well. Most of the nobility, however, lived permanently out in the country along with the vast majority of Russia's people, for Russia remained an overwhelmingly rural land up to the end of the imperial regime.[16]

The privileges of the nobility included a monopoly on the ownership of serfs, nearly unlimited sway over the person and belongings of their serfs, and broad local civil, police, and judicial authority. In other European lands sovereigns had issued codes to regulate the lord-peasant relationship and thereby had limited the power of the nobles. In Russia the only restriction that the law placed upon the serfowner was that the serf "must not suffer ruin" because of the demands of his master. The serfs for their part were ordered by the law to give "silent obedience" to their masters.[17] The serfs became chattels of their owners, subject to their every whim and fancy, bought and sold and gambled away, slaves in everything but name.

In the eighteenth century the nobility had won for itself the exclusive right to the ownership of land. That privilege was eroded in 1801 when Alexander I decreed that any of his subjects, except serfs, could own uninhabited land. In 1848 the law was amended to allow serfs to buy uninhabited land in their own name with the approval of their master.

The nobility also enjoyed exemption from the military draft and freedom from taxes. In 1812 the government introduced a progressive tax on income from landed property. The rate was low and the tax was levied on the basis of an assessment made by the noble landowner himself. Nonetheless, it aroused much hostility among the nobility, which looked upon it as a serious violation of its privilege, and within a few years the tax was repealed.[18]

The special favor enjoyed by the nobility extended beyond the borders of its estates. Noblemen recognized that the growth of the bureaucracy and the increased need for trained officials presented new opportunities for successful careers for their children. Even simple country nobles like the parents of Oblomov in the novel that Goncharov published in 1859 "saw that people could not make their way in life—that is, acquire rank, orders of merit, and money except through education. . . . Sinister rumors were about that not only a knowledge of reading and writing but of other unheard of subjects was required." Enrollment in the secondary schools (*gymnasia*) of the Ministry of Public Instruction rose from 14,000 boys in 1825 to 17,817 in 1855, and the number of such schools rose from sixty to seventy-seven. In 1853, 80 percent of the students belonged to families of the nobility. University enrollments increased from 975 in 1808 to 3,659 in 1855. Comprehensive data are lacking on the social origins of university students, but information for two universities shows a preponderance of nobles. Thus 238 (89 percent) of the 267 students at the University of Kiev in 1838 and 299 (70 percent) of the 424 students at the University of St. Petersburg in 1853 were noble.[19]

The government actively encouraged the near-monopolization of higher education by the sons of the nobility. In 1839 tuition fees were introduced at the universities. In 1845 and again in 1848 the fees were increased. Orders from the Ministry of Public Instruction made admission procedures more difficult for commoners, and in 1850 a decree ordained that each university had to reserve 300 places for the sons of the nobility, because, the decree explained, educated persons of lower social origin "generally become restless citizens, discontented with the established order of things, especially when they cannot give vent for their overexcited ambition."[20]

The value of education as a key to a successful career in government service, combined with the quasi-monopoly of it by the nobility, naturally made it more difficult for men of plebian origin to rise to the highest posts or even to the rank that gave nobility. A study by Walter Pintner of the service records of 2,952 officials who served between the years 1846 and 1855 showed that 2 percent were the sons of merchants and foreigners, 5 percent came from plebian urban and rural families, 20 percent were the sons of priests, 30 percent were the sons of military officers or civil servants who had not attained nobility, and 40 percent were men of noble birth. Moreover, the born nobles held 70 to 80 percent of the highest offices. Family connections and great wealth were significant factors in the ascent to the uppermost ranks. Of the men who reached such rank 18 percent belonged to the 3 percent of noble families who owned more than 500 serfs. Moreover, men with at least one year of university, or who had graduated from one of the elite secondary schools, had almost exclusive possession of the highest offices. There must have been much overlap between these men and the scions of great wealth. However, 42 percent of those in the highest posts had no serfs in their families. They belonged to an hereditary career bureaucracy, with few or no ties to the land.[21]

The success of the nobility in reaching the heights in government service contrasted sharply with its activities in economic life. With rare exceptions, this was a record of stagnation and failure. Instead of using their authority as landowners and serfowners to introduce improvements in their farming operations, nobles contented themselves with doing things the way they had always been done. Some among them did attempt to raise the efficiency and productivity of agriculture. These men were few in number, and even fewer among them met with success. Responsibility for the stagnation of agriculture lay in part with the intractability of the peasants. Departures from traditional routines aroused their suspicion that something was being put over on them, and in any event, like forced and unpaid labor elsewhere in Europe, they were notoriously inefficient. The largest share of the blame, however, fell upon the landowners, who failed to use the power they had to compel their serfs to employ improved methods, and upon the state, which unlike the governments of some other European lands did not provide stimulus and leadership in the adoption of agricultural innovations.

Most nobles who owned land were not market-oriented and did not think in terms of the profitable operations of their estates. They viewed their estates as sources of goods for their own consumption and of money due them by their serfs. Like Oblomov's father they counted it a "divine blessing" if a good harvest or a rise in prices increased their income over the preceding year. Many of them, particularly those in government service, were absentees who left the management of their land to stewards, who often lined their pockets at the expense of their employers. Matters were made worse by the universal testamentary practice, mentioned earlier, of dividing property among all sons. That custom could in a couple of generations splinter a sizable estate into many separate pieces, none of them large enough to support a noble family. Only the existence of vast lands in the colonial regions of the south and east saved all proprietors from this fate. These lands cost little so that many an heir sold his small inheritance to a fellow heir, us d the money to buy land on the frontier, and settled there with his serfs. Efforts to introduce impartible inheritance failed; not even Peter I could force the nobility to accept it. A decree of 1845 allowed the establishment of entails, but set the qualifications so high that only the very wealthiest landowners could make use of the legislation.

The improvidence and economic irrationality of the landowners was actually reinforced by actions of the state. As part of its resolve to protect and sustain the nobility, the government established special banks to lend money to landowners. Since the purpose of these loans, which were secured by mortgages on the serf souls of the borrower, was to keep the nobility in its privileged position, the government rarely foreclosed. It allowed delinquents to remain in possession so that loans often amounted to outright gifts. This leniency invited continuous borrowing. In 1820 one-fifth of all serf souls were mortgaged with state lending institutions. By 1859 two-thirds of all serf souls were so mortgaged. In addition, nobles borrowed heavily from private money lenders. Nearly always they used the money they borrowed for consumption or to pay off old debts, rather than for capital improvements. Many of them spent money with breath-taking profligacy, and even men with seemingly incredible incomes somehow managed to spend more than they received.[22]

Most nobles, encouraged by the government's leniency in advancing them money, showed little concern about the huge indebtedness that rested upon their order. Another policy of the government, however, did awaken their fears and their concern. This was the emancipation of the serfs. The hesitant and half-hearted attempts of Alexander I and Nicholas I to improve the status of the serfs had frightened nobles out of all proportion to their consequences. Then Alexander II, forced by the pressure of events beyond his control, took decisive action and ordered the freeing of the serfs.

Expressions of dismay from the nobility and dire warnings of the dangers of emancipation poured into St. Petersburg, to no avail. Bitter complaints and admonitions proved to be the nobles' only protest. Their dependence upon the throne, their tradition of unquestioning obedience to it, and their lack of experience in corporate action prevented them from doing anything more. With heavy hearts and fears for their own future they followed the orders that they received. A small minority among them supported the emancipation and foretold of benefits that it would bring to landowners. Events soon proved that few prophecies have been more false.

For the emancipation of the serfs in 1861 opened a calamitous last stage in the history of the Russian nobility, during which the pillars upon which its power and privilege had rested crumbled one by one. The first to fall was, of course, its ownership of serfs and its sole right to own inhabited land. In giving up the serfs the nobles lost the goods and services that the serfs had paid. They also had to turn over about half of their land to the now free peasants. They were adequately compensated for these deprivations. But no amount of money could restore to them the world they had lost—a world in which with a minimum of thought and effort they had been housed and clothed and fed and held in respect, and even awe, by the very people who supported them.

Other privileges disappeared, too. In 1874 they lost their exemption from the onerous obligation to supply military recruits. Thereafter noble youths could be drafted into the ranks like any other subject of the tsar for six years of active duty, nine years in the reserve, and five years in the militia. In the mid-1880s nobles lost their exemption from taxation. The gradual abolition of corporal punishment ended another index of rank. In 1762 nobles had gained exemption from such punishment. Twenty years later the exemption had been extended to the order of merchants. Exemption was a measure of privilege and status, for court-ordered whippings were administered not only to punish physically but also to demean. In 1863 townsmen were freed from corporal punishment, and in 1904 so were the peasants. The noble assemblies continued to meet triennially and to elect their marshals and other officials, but imperial legislation reduced still further their already limited area of competence. The continued decline in the authority of the assemblies reduced the small amount of interest that most nobles already had in these bodies. Official data for twenty-six provinces in 1890 showed that out of 276,177 nobles who had the right to attend the provincial assemblies, only 21.3 percent (58,707) appeared.[23]

The division of society into a hierarchy of orders was retained. Men were still legally identified by the order to which they belonged.[24] These forms remained until 1917, but as the years went by and as Russia gradually moved toward civil equality, they were drained of their significance. By the end of the nineteenth century most people seemed no longer interested in knowing the order to which a man belonged, nor did it make any difference whether he was actually enrolled in an order or was legally classified as a *raznochinets*, a man of no particular order.

The nobility did not lose all of its privileges. The laws guaranteed nobles preferential treatment in court proceedings, a special role in preserving law and order at the village level, admission of their children to elite schools, the authority to entail property providing it was above a certain size, and freedom from the quartering of troops. They kept their status symbols, too, such as the right to coats of arms and titles. They also had certain economic privileges that included special rights in distilling and in beet sugar manufacture, exclusive access to the Nobles Bank established in 1885, and perhaps most valuable, a tax rate on land that was about half that levied on peasant land. And, of course, they retained the incalculable advantage of knowing the "right people," and so could use influence to gain favors such as higher initial appointments in the civil service or more rapid promotions than men of nonnoble origin.[25]

In the years immediately following the emancipation some nobles suggested that, as compensation for their relinquishment of serfdom, the political rights of the nobility should be extended without a corresponding expansion of the rights of other orders. Noble assemblies, unhappy about the provisions of the emancipation legislation, petitioned the tsar to summon general convocations to discuss the reworking of the statute. There were requests, too, for the establishment of land mortgage banks modeled after those in Germany and the Austrian Monarchy, to lend money to nobles.[26] These demands went unheeded except that nobles were allowed a greater voice than other orders in the zemstvos, the councils of local government, created in 1864 as one of the "Great Reforms" of Alexander II. The new law required the election of zemstvos in each district, and the district zemstvos, in turn, were to choose the members of provincial zemstvos. The statute divided the electors into three categories and arranged things so that the nobles had the predominant influence, particularly at the provincial level. Initially the reform was applied only to nineteen provinces; by 1875 it had been extended to thirty-four provinces; and by 1914 forty-three of the seventy provinces of the empire had zemstvos. In the mid-1880s 42.4 percent of the deputies to the district zemstvos, and 81.6 percent of those to the provincial ones, belonged to the nobility.[27]

Actually, what happened in the decades after 1861 was not so much a precipitous decline in the status and importance of the nobility, but rather a dilution of its preeminence. Nobles still retained a disproportionate role, in relation to their number, in secondary and higher education, in the bureaucracy, and in the military establishment. A series of reforms had increased the number of, and widened the access to, universities and secondary schools so that student population rose many times over. By 1914 the universities had 35,695 students, and nearly 39,000 more were enrolled in engineering and other technical institutes and specialized academies, such as agricultural and forestry colleges. As could be expected with such a huge increase, the ratio of noble youths dropped sharply. In 1880 the children of hereditary nobles and officials made up 46.6 percent of the student body of the universities; by 1914 that figure had fallen to 36.1 percent.[28] In 1888 in the Vilna school district the children of hereditary nobles comprised 62.9 percent of the enrollment in the gymnasia and pro-gymnasia and 53.3 percent in the *Realschulen*. By 1914 these ratios were 37.3 percent and 25.6 percent, respectively.[29] Nobles, then, no longer held the near-monopoly they once had on university and secondary education, but they were still the single largest social contingent in these institutions.

The expansion of secondary and university education, the great new influx of students from the lower orders, and the growing awareness of western European thought was accompanied by the diffusion of liberal, democratic, and revolutionary ideas among faculty and students. The exposure of young and impressionable nobles to these currents aroused concern among their elders. They decided to establish boarding schools open only to children of the hereditary nobility that would instill traditional values in their pupils along with a good education. The government approved; in March 1891 the Minister of Public Instruction, Count Delianov, called the attention of the provincial governors and of the marshals of the nobility to the need to organize such schools, and by the mid-1890s there were seven of them.[30]

The ever-widening scope of activities of the state and the expanding economy intensified the need for trained specialists of all kinds. The nobility was not large enough, and nobles were often not interested enough or able enough, to meet the demand. So Russian society, of necessity, had to make itself far more open to talent. Merit became increasingly more important than social origin, and more and more men of nonnoble birth ascended to the highest ranks of the bureaucracy and the military establishment. The majority of the closest advisers and leading generals of the last tsar, Nicholas II, men such as Plehve, Giers, Kornilov, Pobedonostsev, Kuropatkin, Alekseev, and Denikin, were commoners by birth, though of course they became nobles as they rose in the Table of Ranks.[31] Nonetheless, at the end of the nineteenth century men born into the nobility still held about 30 percent of the posts in the civil service.[32]

Russia's military forces also expanded, and as with the civil bureaucracy, the nobility could not provide all the officers needed. The officer corps grew from 19,476 in 1864 to 42,777 in 1897. There was more professionalization and a constantly growing need for technically qualified officers. In the old army the customary pattern had been for nobles to serve on active duty for a few years and then to retire. Even when on active duty they often absented themselves from their regiments for long periods. The average length of service during the reign of Nicholas I had been ten years. By the first decade of the 1900s it had lengthened to eighteen years.[33] Nonnoble youths were admitted to the military academies that trained officers (though not until 1913 were all the academies opened to them). Such officers reduced the relative proportion of hereditary nobles in the officer corps. Nonetheless, nobles still comprised a large sector of it. In 1895 a survey of 31,350 officers showed that 50.8 percent (15,938) belonged to families of the hereditary nobility. However, these noble officers were distributed unevenly through the army with the Guards as their special preserve. In 1895, 96.3 percent of the cavalry officers, 90.5 percent of the infantry officers, and 88.7 percent of the artillery officers in the Guards regiments were hereditary nobles. In contrast, in line infantry regiments hereditary nobles made up only 39.6 percent of the officers, and there were regiments that had no hereditary nobles among their officers. Sons traditionally followed fathers into the same Guards regiments, and tradition, too, required them to misuse much of their time in high living and excessive gambling. They had to have private means or an allowance from home to live in what was considered the proper style for a Guards officer, for their pay at best covered a third or less of their expenses. As guardsmen they were stationed in the capital, unlike their less favored fellow officers who spent their careers in provincial posts and on the frontiers, where they had to scratch hard to find attractions that would enliven the monotony of garrison life.

Most of the highest ranking officers apparently belonged to a hereditary career officer caste, much as their analogues in the civil service belonged to a hereditary career bureaucracy. They had few or no ties to the land. As of 1 May 1903 the army had 140 full generals, of whom 10 were members of the imperial family. Data for 80 of the remaining 130 showed that 78 had been born into the nobility. Yet of these 80 full generals 47 (58.7 percent) had no land. Information about 266 lieutenant-generals (out of a total number of 410), of whom 255 (96 percent) were hereditary nobles, revealed that 215 (80.7 percent) were landless. Of 185 major-generals for whom information is available, 159 (86 percent) were hereditary nobles; 168, or over 90 percent, of these men owned no land.[34]

In no sphere was the dilution of noble preeminence so marked and so serious in its consequences to the nobility as it was in agriculture. After emancipation landowners could no longer afford to live without serious regard to income and expenses. Some among them got the message. "Formerly we kept no accounts and drank champagne," one landowner told Mackenzie Wallace a few years after the emancipation, "Now, we keep accounts and content ourselves with beer."[35] But all too few nobles learned that lesson. Instead, the improvidence that had haunted the Russian nobility for so long continued. Nobles also retained the tradition of partible inheritance so that their properties were often reduced in each successive generation.

The emancipation statute had ordered the peasants to compensate the landowners for the land that they relinquished. The state advanced 75 to 80 percent of the cost of the land to the landowners in the form of special government bonds. The peasants were to pay back the state for this advance over a period of forty-nine years. The statute stated that landowners were to be indemnified only for the loss of their land and were to receive nothing for the loss of the person and labor of their erstwhile serfs. However, the state evaded its own legislation by setting the price of the land allotted to the peasant at 20 to 90 percent above its current market price.[36]

It could be expected that the nobles would use the indemnification payments as capital to raise the level of their own agricultural activities. That expectation was never realized. For one thing, the generosity displayed by the government in setting the redemption price of the peasants' allotments was counterbalanced by its deduction from the sums advanced to the nobles of the debts that they owed to state lending institutions. During the first decade after the emancipation that took about 45 percent of the indemnification payments. Secondly, the nobles, always lacking cash, needed it now more than ever to satisfy wants hitherto met by the labor and dues of their serfs. They started selling the redemption bonds and thereby depressed the market for them, so that at times they sold for as little as 70 percent of their par value.[37] Finally, most noble landowners lacked both the knowledge needed to run their estates profitably and the initiative that would have impelled them to gain that knowledge. Their interests lay elsewhere. Those who spent their lives on the land were branded by a contemporary who knew them well as "people not suited for government service, the rejects of the bureaucratic structure." He allowed that rural life sometimes attracted men of talent, but they were "accidents . . . and with their deaths their contributions perished."[38] That harsh judgment was shared by others, including Count Sergei Witte, long-time Minister of Finance (1892–1903) and champion of industrialization, who considered noble landowners incapable of efficient management.[39]

More and more landowners became absentee proprietors. In 1858 one-third of the nobility lived in the cities. By 1897 that ratio had increased to well over one-half (56.9 percent).[40] Many nobles returned to their estates in summer but spent their time in the genteel recreations and the endless visiting so familiar to readers of the great nineteenth-century novels and stories, rather than checking on the operations of their estates. Others abandoned their country homes and allowed them to fall into ruins, like Chertolino, the manor inherited in 1880 by the father of General A. A. Ignatiev. "Like many another estate of the period," Ignatiev wrote in his memoirs, "it was in a condition of complete decay. The best preserved building was the distillery and even that we found without roof and without windows. The old manor house was half burned down, and all the furniture had vanished." Chertolino had 2,500 acres but had only a little more than 100 acres under the plow.[41]

There were some landowners who managed to preserve the patriarchal order and the slow and easy life that they had enjoyed before 1861. They were surrounded by faithful retainers who, knowing no other life, lived out their days serving their old masters. An English traveler in the years before the First World War found that there were many of these "nests of gentlefolk" (so Turgenev called them) out in the countryside. "The house," he wrote, "stands preferably on a river bank or on a hillside. It is half-hidden amidst a grove of trees. Frequently, especially if the house was built, as a great many of the houses of the country gentry were, at the beginning of the nineteenth century, it has a veranda and a balcony supported by massive white columns. Near the house there is sure to be a lime-tree avenue, leading to an orchard of apple, pear, or cherry trees. A flower garden, sometimes with artificial ponds, and a variety of outbuildings complete the number of immediate appurtenances to the manor-house. Indoors, a wide entrance-hall, a big dining room, a drawing room, a kitchen full of busy chattering life, stairs leading to all sorts of quaint nooks and corners, well-stocked store rooms, libraries often containing old and valuable books, pretty, old-fashioned mahogany furniture, family portraits on the wall and generally a snug and soothing sense of leisure, security, and remoteness from the bustle of the world."[42]

Most nobles who engaged in agricultural production used outmoded techniques. That kept their capital outlay at a minimum, but it also kept productive efficiency and their profits at or near minima. The drop in farm prices that began in the 1880s made it even more difficult for them to remain solvent. Many of them gave up farming. In 1886–90 owners of land mortgaged with the Bank of the Nobility had tilled 40 percent of their land on their own account. By the period 1896–1900 that figure had fallen to 29 percent. Meanwhile the amount of their land that they rented out rose from 39 percent to 51 percent.[43] After the turn of the century there were some improvements in techniques, but Russian agriculture still lagged far behind that of other European nations. In the period 1911–1914 capital investment per agricultural worker in Russia amounted to 15 rubles, compared to 130 rubles in neighboring Germany, and average yields in Russia for the chief grains and for potatoes were one-third to one-half those in Germany.[44]

The low return from their estates, their lack of interest in agriculture, and their need for cash persuaded an increasing number of noble landowners to lease or sell their land. They found a ready market; in fact, the demand for land was so strong that it pushed up prices even in periods when grain prices fell. In 1861 the price per desiatin (2.7 acres) averaged out at 17 rubles. By 1895 it had gone up to 77 rubles, and by 1912 it was 163 rubles.[45] The demand came from wealthy townsmen and, above all, from peasants. The townsmen bought land on a large scale in the years immediately after the emancipation. By 1877 they owned nearly 12 million desiatins, and it seemed not impossible that they might ultimately supplant the nobility as the chief landowners of the empire. As land prices soared, their purchases took on a speculative character. Now they bought land for quick and profitable turnovers, while the rate of their permanent acquisitions slowed down.[46]

The peasants, on the other hand, held on to the land that they purchased. The emancipation had not satisfied their land hunger, and their need had escalated with the remarkable increase in their number. Between 1863 and 1913 the rural population in the fifty provinces of European Russia swelled by 87 percent from about 55 millions to 103 millions.[47] Peasants rented land and, when they could, they bought it. By 1881 official data showed that peasants rented 35 percent of the land of estate owners in the fertile black-earth provinces and 29 percent in the rest of Russia. They paid their rents in labor, kind, and cash, with money rents gradually supplanting the other two forms as the cash economy grew.[48] Until the 1880s their purchases of land amounted to less than half that of townsmen. Then in 1883 the government established the Peasant Loan Bank to facilitate purchase of land by the villagers. Just through the financing supplied by this bank alone, peasants by 1913 had bought over 16 million desiatins, or about

67,500 square miles, more land than in all of England, Wales, and
Northern Ireland combined.[49]

Official statistics on landholding reveal the proportions of the decline in landownership by nobles. In 1877 they owned 73 million out
of the 94 million desiatins of land owned by individuals in European
Russia. By 1905 that figure had fallen to 53 million desiatins, a drop of
28 percent, while the area of all individually-owned land had gone up
to 101.7 million desiatins. Meanwhile the amount of land acquired by
individual peasants through purchase increased from 5.8 million desiatins in 1877 to 13.2 million desiatins by 1905. This individually-owned
peasant land was distinct both from the communally-owned allotment
land, the *nadel'nye zemli*, that the peasant communes received through
the operations of the emancipation and from additional land purchased
by the peasant communes in the years after the emancipation. In 1877
the total amount of land owned by peasants individually and com-
munally amounted to 118.2 million desiatins. By 1905 that figure had
risen by over 25 percent to 148.7 million desiatins.[50] In 1861 approximately 128,500 noble families owned land. By 1905 the number had
decreased to 107,200.[51] Nobles had not only lost the near-monopoly
they once had on the ownership of land but now they did not even
hold first place among private landowners. That position belonged to
the peasantry. In 1905 the allotment lands, plus the land purchased by
individual peasants and by peasant communes, made up 63 percent of
all the privately-owned land in the fifty provinces of European Russia.
Nobles owned only 22 percent and townsmen 7 percent.[52]

The nobles did manage to hold on to one valuable natural resource.
They owned most of the forests that were in private hands, and the
emancipation legislation had cancelled most of the rights in these forests that peasants had earlier enjoyed. For many nobles their timber
became their most valuable and their most liquid asset, especially when
after 1880 domestic and foreign demand pushed up lumber prices.
They seized the offers made to them by lumber buyers who roamed
the countryside. Often the seller, like Prince Oblonsky in *Anna
Karenina*, sold at a ridiculously low price because he needed cash in a
hurry to pay for his extravagances and his dissipations.

As in the days of serfdom there were wide disparities in the amount
of land owned by nobles. The following table shows that despite the
overall decline in the number of landowning noble families, those
whose estates were small (under 100 desiatins) increased absolutely as
well as relatively. However, the total amount of land that these small
proprietors owned declined, so that the average size of their holdings
in 1905 was 27 desiatins, compared to 34 in 1877.[53]

		1877		
	Number of noble proprietors	Percentage of total	Area owned (in 1,000s of desiatins)	Percentage of total
Up to 100 desiatins,	56,551	49.3	1,924.4	2.6
101–1,000 desiatins	44,827	34.0	16,264.7	22.2
over 1,000 desiatins	13,388	11.7	54,976.4	75.0
	114,766		73,163.5	
		1905		
Up to 100 desiatins	60,910	56.8	1,662.6	3.1
101–1,000 desiatins	37,003	34.5	13,218.8	24.9
over 1,000 desiatins	9,324	8.7	38,290.9	72.0
	107,237		53,172.3	

Not all nobles lost out in the years after 1861. As the table shows, there was a fairly large minority of middle-sized landowners, and there were still great magnates who owned vast stretches of land. In 1905, 629 landowners each owned over 10,000 desiatins. Of this group 155 had over 50,000 desiatins each, for a total of 16.1 million desiatins, or about one-sixth of all the individually-owned land (101.7 million desiatins) in European Russia. Moreover, nobles acquired additional land through imperial favor. The government sold them land in the western provinces, confiscated from Polish nobles after the rising of 1863, at prices well below market price. Between 1871 and 1881 the government sold nearly half a million desiatins in the frontier provinces of Ufa and Orenburg at an average price of 1.88 rubles per desiatin. Soon thereafter the new owners were selling this land at 60 rubles per desiatin. Other distributions of land brought the total made available to nobles up to about 2 million desiatins by 1890. Some of the great nobles also owned large industrial establishments that included mining and metallurgical enterprises in the Urals and beet sugar factories in the Ukraine. Others, large and small, were active as grain traders. Some nobles owned large tracts of urban property that brought mounting returns as cities grew; and some bought shares in Russian industries and banks—the wealthiest among these had millions invested by 1914.[54]

The continued prosperity of the fortunate few could not conceal the general decline in wealth and status of the nobility. The decline became a matter of concern to the autocracy. To reverse it became a central policy of the government of Alexander III, whose accession in 1881 ushered in an era of militant and ruthless reaction. The concern about the nobility did not spring from a fatherly solicitude of the tsar. The throne had always relied upon the nobility to carry out its policies, and the nobility had never failed it. Now, more than ever before, the throne needed its loyal nobility to help it meet the challenge to autocratic rule that issued from economic advances and from new and disturbing social and political ideas. The new tsar, a narrow-minded and poorly educated bigot, surrounded himself with advisers who shared his conviction that the forces of change had to be shackled. The restoration of the nobility to its former preeminence was an essential part of their strategy.

Alexander III in his coronation speech in 1883, and especially in his rescript issued on the one hundredth anniversary of the Charter of the Nobility in 1885, set the tone for his new policy. He spoke of the natural superiority of the nobility (the belief that nobles were more honorable and more virtuous than ordinary mortals was part of the mythology of every society of orders), promised to protect the nobility's economic position, and expressed his hope that, as in the past, nobles would maintain "their role of leaders in war, in matters of local government and justice, in unselfish concern for the needs of the people, and by their example [would] spread the precepts of religion, of loyalty, and the sound principles of popular education."[55]

The establishment of the Land Bank for the Nobility in 1885 turned out to be the most successful of the efforts on behalf of the nobility undertaken by Alexander's government. Nobles had complained since 1861 of their need for cheap credit and had urged the establishment by the government of an institution that would provide this. The new bank answered their demands. It made generous loans at an interest rate (4½ percent, later reduced to 4 percent) that was well below that charged by other lenders. Nobles, large and small, hastened to borrow against their properties, and when the increase in land prices increased the value of their properties they came back for second and third mortgages. Most of them applied their loans to unproductive uses, and soon arrears piled up. In the period 1906–1908 the delinquency rate on annual payments stood at 60.7 percent; in 1913 it was 40.6 percent. The bank's purpose, like that of its predecessor in the days of serfdom, was to save nobles from losing their land. So foreclosures were rare. Between 1906 and 1913 only 400 properties out of 28,000 mortgaged with the bank were sold to satisfy loans. Nobles also borrowed heavily from private banks, and those who found themselves especially hard-pressed turned to usurers who charged them high rates.[56]

The creation in 1889 of the office of land captain (*zemskii nachal'nik*) proved to be a less successful innovation. This reform was intended to restore to the nobility its authority in the countryside. The law ordered the division of each county (*uezd*) into districts, usually four or five, each of which was to have a land captain. The captain was nominated by the local noble assembly, preferably from among the local nobility, and was appointed by the Ministry of the Interior under whose supervision he held his office. The law gave the land captains extensive powers over the peasants—powers that were reminiscent of the days of serfdom. Events quickly demonstrated that the new office was ill-suited for the task assigned to it, and soon new laws took away some of the more arbitrary powers of the land captain. Personnel problems proved troublesome, too. Often a noble suitable for the post could not be found in the district, sometimes because all the capable men had moved to the cities and sometimes because the salary was too low to attract competence. In such cases the government had to appoint a nonnoble or assign one of its bureaucrats to the post. Finally, in 1906, as part of the legislation that swept away many of the legal disabilities of the peasantry, the land captains were stripped of most of their authority.[57]

Encouraged by the pronoble attitude of the government, representatives of the landed nobility pressed for further favorable legislation. In this they had little success. To be sure, special commissions on noble affairs were established. In 1891 Alexander appointed one of them, but nothing came of its lengthy discussions that lasted through most of 1892.[58] A few years later Alexander's son and successor, Nicholas II, ordered the convening of a Special Conference for the Affairs of the Nobility. At one of its first sessions in 1897 the conference, whose members included provincial marshals of the nobility, expressed its opposition to the participation in the assemblies of the nobility of men who had "lost all ties with the land and who live in the world of money and bureaucratic interests, far distant from the real needs of our provincial life."[59] Nothing came of that resolution, nor, apparently, of anything else discussed by the conference in the five years of its existence.

One of Alexander's reactionary policies concerned the zemstvos. Apparently, his government felt that the already preponderant influence of the nobility in these councils needed strengthening. In 1890 new legislation increased noble representation, so that nobles came to make up 55.2 percent and 89.5 percent, respectively, of the district and provincial zemstvos. As things turned out, however, these changes had the opposite effect to that desired. From 1866 the government, concerned by the threat to its autocratic rule of zemstvo autonomy, steadily reduced the authority of these bodies. This weakening discouraged many nobles, already skeptical of the value of the zemstvos, from participating in them. This apathy allowed a liberal minority (a Soviet historian called them "bourgeoisified" nobles) to gain much influence. It also allowed greater freedom for the professional employees of the zemstvos, the doctors, teachers, lawyers, agronomists, statisticians, and so on, who often had liberal or leftist political convictions. So instead of becoming supports of the reaction, the zemstvos provided the organizational base for noble discontent and even opposition to the autocracy.[60] After the turn of the century zemstvo leaders defied governmental displeasure and held conferences that became the chief organs of liberal noble opinion. In November 1904 a conference of a hundred leaders from thirty-three provinces, by an overwhelming majority, adopted an eleven-point resolution that included demands for civil liberties, equality before the law, and the summoning of a representative legislative assembly.

Among the liberal nobles were professional men, scholars, littérateurs, bureaucrats, and even some landowners who belonged to that peculiarly Russian phenomenon, the *intelligentsia*. These men and women were more likely to identify with their fellow *intelligents* than with their fellow nobles. And, of course, there was the small number of nobles, most of them young and university-educated, who were completely alienated from their society and belonged to radical groups dedicated to the overthrow of the regime. These youthful radicals reminded Leroy-Beaulieu in the 1880s of the French nobles of the *ancien régime* who were drawn to the radical ideologies of that day. "As long as revolutionary ideas retain something speculative about them," he wrote, "as long as they are not able to be put into practice, they easily find partisans among the very classes who are destined to become their victims."[61]

The discontent of liberal nobles with the autocracy, like the revolutionary zeal of the radicals, was external evidence of the changes that were transforming Russia. Industrialization, railroads, the growth of cities, expanded education, and the increased knowledge and envy of Western liberal and democratic institutions undermined the traditional order. These subversive forces, reinforced by governmental ineptitude and military defeat, brought on the revolutionary storm of 1905. Frightened by the turn of events, Tsar Nicholas by his manifesto of October 17 transformed autocratic Russia into a constitutional monarchy. But the revolutionary tide soon ebbed, and by late 1906 the throne had regained much that it had yielded only a year before, though it could not wholly return to the way things had been. Too many irreversible changes had taken place.

One change, however, did prove reversible. Nobles who in the zemstvos, and then during the revolutionary fever of 1905 in provincial assemblies, had demanded representative government and universal and equal suffrage made a complete about-face. They abandoned their brief flirtation with revolution and took up their traditional role as the chief prop of the throne and the supporter of its reactionary policies. The explanation for the turnabout is easy to find: the threat of land reform and land expropriation. The long-simmering discontent of the peasantry had erupted in 1905, and again in 1906, into open defiance and violence. That badly frightened the landowning nobility. Then the elections to the First and Second Dumas in 1906 and 1907 returned many peasant delegates who were committed to the compulsory alienation (with compensation) of the landowners' property, to satisfy the land hunger of their constituents. They had the support of the delegates of the liberal Constitutional Democrats, the Cadets, many of whom were of landowning families but who were intimidated by the spectre of mass peasant risings.

To stave off the threat of expropriation and to preserve domestic order, nobles turned to political activism. They associated themselves with the new political parties and the pressure groups that appeared with the establishment of constitutional government in Russia. Many of them favored the conservative Octobrist party. Others supported the extreme right, and notably the Union of the Russian People. That sinister and obscene mass movement drew its membership from all levels of society. Dedicated to the restoration of the autocracy and favored by the regime, it openly engaged in criminal activities included assassinations and pogroms without fear of punishment. Tsar Nicholas hailed the organization as "the mainstay of the throne" and "the standard bearer of legality and order."[62] Nobles also formed their own organization, the Council of the United Nobility, in 1906 as a vehicle through which they could exert political pressure on the government in matters that affected their interests. The United Nobility seized upon every opportunity to check the advances of constitutional government and of civil rights, as threats to the privileges and property of the nobility. It urged the forceful suppression of revolutionary activity and backed the government's use of field-courts-martial to crush radicalism. It was influential in bringing about the revision of the electoral laws that was ordered by the imperial decree of 3 June 1907. That decree enabled the nobility, who formed less than 1 percent of the population, to hold more than half the seats in the Third and Fourth Dumas. It gave strong support to the so-called Stolypin reforms that allowed enterprising peasants to leave the village community and establish themselves as private proprietors. Once nobles had looked upon the commune as a guarantee against the emergence of a landless proletariat. Now they saw it as a launching pad for socialism and so they favored its dissolution.

The zemstvos, too, only shortly ago leaders in the demands for civil rights and constitutional government, became instruments of noble reaction. In the first zemstvo elections held after the Revolution of 1905 the liberals who had dominated these councils suffered crushing defeats. Most of the zemstvos came under the control of conservative and reactionary nobles. These men used their position to block reform at the local level and to discharge many zemstvo employees because they often were partisans of leftist and revolutionary movements.[63]

Thus the nobility, in league with the throne, beat off the attacks on its land and its status. Its victory, however, was short lived, snuffed out by war and revolution. But even if Russia and the world had been spared those twin catastrophes it seems unlikely that the nobility would have been able to sustain its conquest of its enemies. Despite its political success after 1905 it continued its downward glide. Contemporaries, including nobles, recognized this. Some members of the United Nobility described themselves as aurochs, representatives of a dying species. The epithet caught on with press and public, for it aptly expressed the general attitude toward the nobility.[64] In 1914 Maurice Baring, who knew old Russia well, wrote that the nobility there "is being slowly and gradually oozed out of existence; it is being subjected to a slow process of expropriation in favor of the peasants, the merchants, and the new capitalists; and in the course of time . . . the nobility as a caste of landowners will disappear altogether."[65] Years later V. A. Maklakov, himself a nobleman and moderate member of the Cadet party, in reminiscing about the expropriation bills introduced in the First Duma, asked "Why was it necessary to destroy the class of private landowners by an accelerated method, by political action, instead of letting it die a natural death?"[66]

But why was it going to die a natural death? Why was it slowly being oozed out of existence? Why with the advantages given it by its preferments and privileges was it unable to adjust and survive? A number of answers to these questions suggest themselves. Some are historical stereotypes such as the victory of the capitalistic mode of production over "feudal" society, or, to put it another way, the "bourgeoisification" of the nobility. Those who eschew the rhetoric of the dialectic refer to the disintegration of old Russia brought on by the advances of industry and transportation, by urbanization, by education, and by the penetration of Western ideas about society and government. At another level the decline of the nobility can be explained as the consequence of the transition from a society of orders to the modern class society. In the society of orders a person's status, rights, and duties depended upon the order into which he was born or into which he ascended or descended. In the modern class society a person's status depends upon his economic role. As Sombart pointed out,[67] in the traditional society the possession of wealth had been the consequence of the possession of power and privilege. In the modern society the possession of power and privilege becomes the consequence of the possession of wealth.

Each of these answers has much to recommend it. Worrisome difficulties appear, however, when the Russian experience is compared with that of other European lands. They, too, experienced the trauma of modernization, and to a greater degree than did Russia. Yet in those lands the nobility not only survived but maintained its preeminence far more successfully than did the nobles of Russia. A more satisfactory answer has to include circumstances that were peculiar to the Russian nobility.

As earlier pages have noted, the Russian nobility, unlike its peers in other lands, had no territorial base from which it could draw authority and resolution and a sense of independence. Instead, the Russian nobility was subservient to and dependent upon the throne. The final decisions lay always with the throne; the nobles had no ultimate responsibility. To compensate them for their loyal dependence and to assure for them a comfortable way of life with a minimum of effort, the autocracy gave them great power over their peasants. If they still had difficulties in making ends meet, the autocracy lent them large sums of money without insisting upon repayment.

I suggest that this parasitic dependence of the nobility upon the throne bred men who lacked initiative and drive, or channeled the initiative and creativity that they did possess into directions other than the preservation of their estates. For many of them irresponsibility and prodigality became a way of life. When in 1861 they lost their serfs and half their lands, they felt themselves lost. Suddenly they found themselves shut out of the life they had known for so long and in which they had been so content. One stroke of the tsar's pen had wiped out their role in the rural world, and they seemed incapable of adjusting. The long decades of dependence during which the tsars had pampered and protected them had sapped them of the instinct for survival. Their loss of peasants and land was not unique. That had happened to the nobles of Germany and of the Austrian Monarchy only a few years earlier. What was unique was the inability of the Russian nobles to recover from the blow, unlike the elite of central Europe, of whom many had actually welcomed the abolition of the

old lord-peasant relationship. Instead of reaching out for the opportunities presented by the changing society in which they lived, the
Russian nobility tried to hold on to their obsolete values while their
land, their wealth, and their power steadily slipped away from them.

It is impossible to document an indictment of an entire social order.
Fortunately, there are sources which provide much supporting evidence: the great Russian novels and plays and short stories of the
nineteenth century. "The central category and criterion of realist literature," wrote George Lukács, "is the type, a peculiar synthesis
which organically binds together the general and the particular both
in characters and situations. What makes a type a type is not its
average quality, nor its mere individual being, however profoundly
conceived; what makes it a type is that in it all the humanly and
socially essential determinants are present at their highest level of development. . . ."[68] The geniuses of Russian literature, nearly all of
them born into the hereditary nobility, presented their characters as
individuals and at the same time gave them the dimensions of general
types having historical validity. "*The Hero of our Time*," wrote
Lermontov in 1840 in the preface to the second edition of his novel, "is
certainly a portrait, but not of a single person. It is a portrait of the
vices of our whole generation in its ultimate development."

To the historian of the nobility the most striking of these types is
that of the "superfluous man," to use Turgenev's famed epithet. Time
and again the reader meets landowners who, seemingly attired always
in dressing gown, pass their days in useless activities or simply in
wasting time, like Onegin's uncle who spent forty years berating his
housekeeper and squashing flies, and whose only book was an 1808
almanac without a binding. Some, like Onegin himself, lived in the
midst of high society and great wealth. Others, like Goncharov's
Oblomov or Turgenev's Rudin or the superfluous man who is the
diarist in Turgenev's story, lived out their lives in obscurity. Some,
like Onegin or Lermontov's Pechorin, engaged in futile activity in the
never realized hope of escaping the terrible boredom that clouded
their lives. Others, like Oblomov or Gogol's Tentetnikov, spent their
days in apathy and indolence, dreaming of a perfect life in which their
every want would be satisfied with absolutely no effort on their part,
or meditating about a great scholarly treatise, but never writing a
word. The Oblomovs and the Tentetnikovs felt no guilt, but more
sensitive men like Onegin or Pechorin or Tolstoi's Prince Nekhludov
or Konstantin Levin are torn by inner struggles and indecision in their
effort to justify to themselves their way of life.

The improvidence, the prodigality, and the ineptitude that brought disaster to noble families are recounted time and again. Nowhere is it more poignantly and memorably told than in *The Cherry Orchard*, Chekhov's last and greatest play. The members of the family lack the will to solve, or even to meet, the problems of their personal lives, much less their common economic problem. They recoil in horror from the suggestion that they sell the orchard. Yet they have no alternative, for they are too irresolute to take any action save to continue their aimless and useless lives, though they know ruin will soon overtake them. The thud of the axe as it fells the trees in the orchard provides the melancholy epitaph for the elite of old Russia.

NOTES

1. M. Baring, *The Mainsprings of Russia* (London, 1914), p. 82.
2. A. Romanovich-Slavatinskii, *Dvorianstvo v Rossii ot nachala XVIII veka do otmeny krepostnago prava* (St. Petersburg, 1870), pp. 38–41.
3. A. Leroy-Beaulieu, *L'empire des tsars et les russes* (Paris, 1883), 1: 341–42.
4. Quoted in A. P. Korelin, "Rossiiskoe dvorianstvo i ego soslovnaia organizatsiia (1861–1904 gg.)," *Istoriia SSSR*, no. 5, 1971, 65.
5. "Dvorianstvo" in F. Brockhaus and I. Efron, eds., *Entsiklopedicheskii Slovar*.
6. Korelin, p. 60.
7. Number of nobles from A. P. Korelin, "Dvorianstvo v poreformennoi Rossii," *Istoricheskie Zapiski*, no. 87, 1971, pp. 124, 129–35. Population in 1858 is from Tsentral'nyi Statisticheskii Komitet, *Statisticheskiia tablitsy Rossiiskoi Imperii* (St. Petersburg, 1863). Population in 1897 is from *Statisticheskiia svedeniia po zemel'nomu voprosu v Evropeiskoi Rossii* (St. Petersburg, 1906).

In France on the eve of the 1798 revolution nobles made up 1–1½ percent of the population (A. Soboul, *La France à la veille de la Révolution* [Paris, 1960], 1: 40–41); in Poland before the partitions 8–10 percent of the people were noble, and in Spain in 1787 about 5 percent (M. S. Anderson, *Europe in the Eighteenth Century* [New York, 1961], p. 40); in Hungary in the 1820s nobles made up about 4 percent of the population (G. Barany, *Stephen Széchenyi and the Awakening of Hungarian Nationalism, 1791–1841* [Princeton, 1968], p. 149).
8. M. N. Korkunov, *Russkoe gosudarstvennoe pravo* (St. Petersburg, 1893), 1: 206–11.
9. D. M. Wallace, *Russia* (New York, 1878), p. 281.
10. Romanovich-Slavatinskii, pp. 58–61.
11. K. Ruffmann, "Russischer Adel als Sondertypus der europäischen Adelswelt," *Jahrbücher für Geschichte Osteuropas* 9 (1961): 167; *Polnoe sobranie zakonov Rossiiskoi Imperii*, ser. 2, vol. 31, no. 31236.
12. M. Raeff, *Michael Speransky, Statesman of Imperial Russia 1772–1839* (The Hague, 1957), pp. 44–45, 234; V. I. Gurko, *Features and Figures of the Past* (Stanford, 1939), p. 204; J. Engelmann, *Die Leibeigenschaft in Russland* (Leipzig, 1884), pp. 283–84.

Despite the instructions of the Charter of the Nobility, not all hereditary nobles had access to these assemblies. None were organized in sparsely populated provinces where there were few nobles, and the assemblies in nine western provinces were suspended after 1863 because the Polish nobles there had taken part in the Polish rising of that year. In all, thirty-five provinces, containing about 60 percent of the hereditary nobility, had assemblies. Korelin, "Rossiiskoe dvorianstvo," p. 58.

13. Romanovich-Slavatinskii, pp. 24, 43–46.

14. A. G. Troinitskii, *Krepostnoe naselenie v Rossii po 10–ii narodnoi perepisi* (St. Petersburg, 1861), p. 67.

15. Ia. A. Solov'ev, "Zapiski Senatora Ia. A. Solov'eva o krest'ianskom dele," *Russkaia Starina* 30 (1881): 746–47.

16. In 1863, 90 percent of Russia's population was rural; 84.8 percent still was rural in 1914. A. G. Rashin, *Naselenie Rossii za 100 let, 1811–1913* (Moscow, 1956), p. 98. In 1911 in France 55.9 percent, in 1913 in Germany 25.8 percent, and in 1911 in Great Britain only 11.5 percent of the population were rural. B. H. Slicher van Bath, "The Influence of Economic Conditions on the Development of Agricultural Tools and Machines in History," in J. L. von Meij, ed., *Mechanization in Agriculture* (Amsterdam, 1960), p. 19; H. See, *Histoire économique de la France* (Paris, 1939–1951), 2: 328.

17. *Svod zakonov Rossiiskoi Imperii*, 1857 ed., sect. 1029, 1045.

18. J. Blum, *Lord and Peasant in Russia* (Princeton, 1961), pp. 361–62; Raeff, p. 104.

19. N. Hans, *History of Russian Educational Policy, 1701–1917* (London, 1931), pp. 29, 235–36, 238; W. H. E. Johnson, *Russia's Educational Heritage* (New Brunswick, 1950), table 19.

20. Hans, pp. 77–78.

21. W. M. Pintner, "The Social Characteristics of the Early Nineteenth-Century Russian Bureaucracy," *Slavic Review* 29 (1970): 434–40.

22. Blum, pp. 376–85.

23. Korelin, "Rossiiskoe dvorianstvo," pp. 80–81.

24. Cf. the trial scene in bk. 1, chap. 9 of Tolstoi's *Resurrection*.

25. "Dvorianstvo" in F. Brockhaus and I. Efron, ed., *Entsiklopedicheskii Slovar*; L. Martov, P. Maslov, A. Potresov, eds., *Obshchestvennoe dvizhenie v' Rossii v' nachale XX-go veka* (St. Petersburg, 1909–1911), 1: 164; Korelin, "Rossiiskoe dvorianstvo," p. 57.

26. A. A. Kornilov, *Modern Russian History*, (New York, 1943), 2: 70–74; S. F. Starr, *Decentralization and Self-Government in Russia, 1830–1870* (Princeton, 1972), pp. 235–37, 245–46.

27. P. A. Zaionchkovskii, *Rossiiskoe samoderzhavie v kontse XIX stoletiia* (Moscow, 1970), p. 410.

28. Hans, pp. 238–40. The ratio of the children of the lower urban order rose from 12.4 percent in 1880 to 24.3 percent in 1914; that of peasant children from 3.3 percent to 14.5 percent in the same years.

29. D. M. Odinetz and P. J. Novgorotsev, *Russian Schools and Universities in the World War* (New Haven, 1929), p. 33.

30. Korelin, "Rossiiskoe dvorianstvo," p. 70.

31. Gurko, p. 203.

32. Korelin, Russiiskoe dvorianstvo," p. 70.

33. Korelin, "Dvorianstvo v poreformennoi Rossii," pp. 156–57; R. L. Garthoff, "The Military as a Social Force," in C. E. Black, ed., *The Transformation of Russian Society* (Cambridge, Mass., 1960), pp. 325, 327. Apparently, despite the increased professionalization, officers continued to absent themselves for long periods while on active duty yet were counted as present. A. A. Ignatiev, *A Subaltern in Old Russia* (London, 1944), p. 73.

34. P. A. Zaionchovskii, "Soslovnyi sostav ofitserskogo korpusa na rubezhe xix–xx vekov," *Istoriia SSSR*, no. 1, 1973, 148–52.

35. Wallace, p. 517.

36. A. Gerschenkron, "Agrarian Policies and Industrialization: Russia 1861–1917," *Cambridge Economic History of Europe* (Cambridge, 1965) 6: 738–39.

37. P. I. Liashchenko, *Istoriia narodnogo khoziaistva SSSR* (Moscow, 1952), 1:

600; G. Pavlovsky, *Agricultural Russia on the Eve of the Revolution* (London, 1930), 100.

38. A. A. Mertago quoted in A. M. Anfimov, *Krupnoe pomeshchich'e khoziaistvo evropeiskoi Rossii* (Moscow, 1969), p. 290.

39. Gurko, p. 202.

40. Korelin, "Dvorianstvo v poreformennoi Rossii," p. 169.

41. Ignatiev, p. 25.

42. H. W. Williams, *Russia of the Russians* (London, 1914), p. 363.

43. Pavlovsky, pp. 104, 111, 190–91.

44. Anfimov, pp. 83, 182–83, 373–75.

45. Ibid., p. 358.

46. G. T. Robinson, *Rural Russia under the Old Regime* (New York, 1932) pp. 132–33.

47. Rashin, p. 98.

48. Pavlovsky, pp. 106–8.

49. Anfimov, p. 318.

50. Tsentral'nyi Statisticheskii Komitet, *Statistika zemlevladenie 1905g. Svod dannykh po 50-ti guberniiam evropeiskoi Rossii* (St. Petersburg, 1907), table 2, pp. 12, 16–17, table 3, pp. 78–79, table 5, pp. 130–31.
In 1905 land owned by private individuals (noble or peasant) and land owned collectively by the peasants made up 60.9 percent of all land in the fifty provinces of European Russia. The rest belonged to the state, the church, and other institutions.

51. Korelin, "Dvorianstvo v poreformennoi Rossii," pp. 139–40, 150–51.

52. Tsentral'nyi statisticheskii komitet, *Statistika zemlevladenie 1905g.* p. 11, appendix tables 3–9.

53. N. A. Proskuriakova, "Razmeshchenie i struktura dvorianskogo zemlevladeniia evropeiskoi Rossii v kontse xix- nachale xx veka," *Istoriia SSSR*, no. 1, 1973, 68.

54. Anfimov, pp. 28–31, 255–86, 357; Korelin, "Dvorianstvo v poreformennoi Rossii," pp. 163–64.

55. Quoted in Korelin, "Rossiiskoe dvorianstvo," p. 76.

56. Anfimov, pp. 318, 323–27.

57. B. Pares, *Russia and Reform* (1907; reprint ed., Westport Conn., 1973), p. 120; G. L. Yaney, *The Systematization of Russian Government* (Urbana, 1973), pp. 312, 269–70; Gurko, pp. 146–47.

58. Iu. B. Solov'ev, "Pravitel'stvo i politika ukrepleniia klassovnykh pozitsii dvorianstva v kontse xix veka," in N. E. Nosov et al., ed., *Vnutrenniaia politika tsarizma* (Leningrad, 1967), pp. 240–41.

59. Quoted in Korelin, "Rossiiskoe dvorianstvo," p. 65.

60. Zaionchkovskii, *Rossiiskoe samoderzhavie* pp. 410–11, 434; G. Fisher, *Russian Liberalism from Gentry to Intelligentsia* (Cambridge, Mass., 1958), pp. 11–13. As pointed out in an earlier page, in the mid-1860s nobles had comprised 42.4 percent and 81.8 percent of the district and provincial zemstvos, respectively.

61. Leroy-Beaulieu, 1: 374–75.

62. M. T. Florinsky, *Russia: a History and an Interpretation* (New York, 1953), p. 1201.

63. B. Veselovskii, "Dvizhenie zemlevladel'tsev'," in Marov, Maslov, and Potresov, vol. 1, pt. 2, pp. 11–14, 29; A. Levin, *The Second Duma*, 2nd ed. (Hamden, Conn., 1966), pp. 237–38; Robinson, pp. 181–83.

64. Williams, p. 371. The aurochs is the extinct European wild ox.

65. Baring, p. 89.

66. V. Maklakov, *The First State Duma* (Bloomington, 1964), p. 142.

67. W. Sombart, *Der moderne Kapitalismus* (Munich and Leipzig, 1928), vol. 1, pt. 2, p. 586.

68. G. Lukács, *Studies in European Realism* (New York, 1964), p. 6.

RICHARD HERR

5 | Spain

To take up the case of Spain in a volume dedicated to investigating
how European landed elites coped with the new and alien forces of the
nineteenth century places one at the outset in a quandary. What the
subject brings immediately to mind is not a Spanish scene. Rather it
recalls the picture of the English landholding aristocracy, entrenched
in control of Parliament after 1688 and strengthened economically by
the enclosure movement, faced with the rise of a wealthy industrial
class and with a series of parliamentary reforms that threaten its political hegemony. Or it makes one think of the French aristocracy,
flushed with successful resistance to the crown's attempt to reform the
tax structure in the eighteenth century and strengthened by reassert-
ing old privileges, falling victim to the democratic drive of the French
Revolution, losing its privileges, losing part of its lands, and swamped
in the long run by a new bourgeois society and egalitarian constitution. It may even suggest the plantation owners of the American South
attacked by self-righteous abolitionists and northern factory owners
and eventually defeated in civil war. On a theoretical level, the subject
seems inspired by the materialist dialectic, with its prognosis of the
inevitable displacement of the feudal class by the capitalist bourgeoisie.

All of these images illustrate the subject of landed elites struggling
with new and alien forces, but none of them has its setting in Spain.
What Spanish picture can we fit to it? What, in Spain, were the
threatening forces of the nineteenth century? There was no French
Revolution, no great industrial revolution; there were various civil
wars, but none that so clearly pitted different social systems against
each other as the American Civil War. And what was the "landed
elite"? This last question sounds simpler, for at least we know that
Spain was largely an agricultural country. Let us start with it.

"Elite" implies, of course, a select group. On what grounds shall we select among all the people who owned land in Spain, from the king to the smallest peasant? To say those with the most land does not tell us who they were. The aristocracy appears the most obvious group. In Spain this would be those nobles who had titles; for references to the Spanish aristocracy are never meant to include simple *hidalgos*, who, though noble, had only the title "don." In 1787 there were 119 *grandes* and 535 other titled nobles, a total of about 650 aristocrats.[1] This number grew considerably in the nineteenth century. Jaime Vicens Vives has charted the frequency with which the monarchs gave new titles. The number of grants increased during or following periods of turmoil (150 titles were given out in the 1870s, in response to the revolution of 1868 and the First Republic).[2] The monarchs used titles to reward their influential supporters and to win the allegiance of military, political, and entrepreneurial leaders. By 1896 the number of aristocrats had risen to 207 grandes and 1206 other titled nobles, roughly double the figure of 1787.[3]

Many of the new aristocrats were not primarily landowners, however much they may have desired social acceptance by the old landed families. In 1932 the Cortes of the Second Republic ordered the confiscation without compensation of those properties of the grandes which fell into the categories of land subject to expropriation under the Republic's agrarian reform law. (The law was complex. The origin of the title, the quality of the land, its current use, and extent within individual municipal boundaries were all taken into account in determining the amount an owner was permitted to keep; but the limits were conceived to eliminate the unjust economic and political advantage accruing to owners of large holdings.[4]) The confiscation applied only to those grandes who had exercised the honorific privileges of their rank (that is, were adults and active at court); these were 176 of the current total of 262 grandes. Of these 176 only 99 owned any expropriable property. The rest may have owned land, but not in large enough blocks for the republicans to consider their properties incompatible with a democratic system and they therefore seem hardly to qualify for inclusion in the landed elite. Furthermore, of the 99 subject to expropriation, 24 owned less than 500 hectares of expropriable property. Thus only 75 out of 176 adult, active grandes in 1932 (43 percent) were owners of truly major holdings.[5]

An analysis of the list of expropriable grandes shows that on the average those whose titles dated from the nineteenth century owned less land than the older aristocrats, as one would expect.[6] Even families who had entered the aristocracy before 1800, however, did not form a solid landed class. A quarter of them had less than 500 hectares of expropriable property in 1932, if they had any at all. Some had disposed of lands since 1800, but we do not know how many.

Thus we cannot use the aristocracy, even the old aristocracy, as a synonym for the landed elite. To make possible a rational analysis of nineteenth-century developments, let me for the moment define the landed elite not simply as those persons who owned the largest properties but as those whose ownership or control of the land was such that others who made their living from the land were put in a position of dependency on them or subjection to them. This is an abstract and structural definition, and very imprecise at that, but it is clear that there were real people who fitted the definition. The problem is that we have virtually no studies that permit us to visualize them directly.[7]

We can, however, approach the question indirectly. We have descriptions of the upper levels of rural society in the eighteenth century and in the early twentieth century. From them one can interpolate the evolution that took place in the nineteenth century. The first description derives from a famine of the 1760s that had provoked serious urban riots throughout Spain.[8] The government of Charles III called upon the provincial intendants and other officials of the grain-producing areas of the crown of Castile to report on the nature of local landowning and propose reforms that would increase output. Besides being familiar with their provinces, these officials could refer to a complete cadastral survey or *catastro* of property and income that had been carried out in the 1750s as a prerequisite for a projected reform of the tax structure. Their reports became the basis for a series of proposals for agrarian reform that culminated in 1795 in the *Informe de Ley Agraria*, written by Spain's most acute thinker of the century, the royal councilor Gaspar Melchor de Jovellanos.[9]

The royal reformers stressed the evil of vast inequality in the ownership of property, and they blamed it primarily on the legal privilege of entail. Ecclesiastical institutions by accepted right and private individuals by specific legal act of *vinculación* tied up their property so that it could not be sold, at least not without complicated petitions for specific royal authorization. Blocks of land of varying size thus became the inalienable property of churches and monasteries, and also of aristocratic, hidalgo, and even common families. The cadastral survey showed that ecclesiastical institutions owned about 20 percent of the land of Castile, measured by the value of the harvests and pastures. Lay *vínculos*, known frequently as *mayorazgos*, probably included more property, but much less than the extravagant claims that have sometimes been made.[10]

Inequality was greatest in the southern part of Castile: La Mancha,

Extremadura, and Andalusia. Here aristocrats and military orders had large seigneurial jurisdictions (*señoríos*), with the right to appoint certain municipal officials and collect certain dues. Señorío often included the control of the town lands, giving the *señor* the profit from extensive pastures. The señor of the towns of the military orders was the king, but the income from these jurisdictions went also to the *caballeros* of the orders, who were aristocrats and prominent hidalgos.

In southern Spain, besides extensive estates in pasture, there were large grain-growing properties called *cortijos*. The mayorazgos of aristocrats normally included cortijos, often within their señoríos. Hidalgos owning cortijos and other large properties were, however, far more important numerically than aristocrats. They also had more influence in local affairs, for most aristocrats were absentee owners. Hidalgos tended to dominate the municipal councils through the ownership of the hereditary offices of *regidor*. The cadastral survey reveals, for example, that in the Andalusian town of Baños (Jaén province) three extended hidalgo families, which included seven male heads of household, two widows, and a single woman, dominated the social structure because of their extensive income from landed property. Four of the men were regidores, two were other town officials, and the seventh was the local officer of the Inquisition. The town curate and a man in minor orders, both individually wealthy, also belonged to these families. We should class this kind of hidalgo among the elite, along with aristocratic señores. There were several other noble families in Baños of decreasing affluence and influence. Where one should draw the line below which the hidalgos of Baños and other Andalusian towns were no longer elite would be difficult to determine.[11]

Two other groups belonged to the elite. First were the clergy who, although they were not individual landowners, drew income directly from ecclesiastical landholdings. One form of income was the endowed benefices, the *capellanías*. Their holders included priests, many of them without a cure, cathedral canons, inquisitors, even university professors. Most of these did not reside where the lands whose income they enjoyed were located. Many impersonal institutions also had large holdings: monasteries, shrines, cathedrals, hospitals, and other associations of the faithful. In this case the clergy responsible for them, while not drawing direct income, nevertheless profited indirectly and had economic influence over numerous peasants who rented or worked the lands.

While the cadastral survey shows that in Castile the church owned property producing about 20 percent of the total income from land, the extent of ecclesiastical landholding varied widely from place to place. In Baños the figure was only 14 percent, but in the northeastern part of the province of Salamanca, a rich region of two-and-three-field farming mixed with larger grazing properties, 47 percent of the income from land went to religious institutions. Here, in a pattern more typical of the northern part of Castile, the economic power of the church was based on the ownership of a large number of tiny plots which were leased to local peasants.[12]

The other group belonging to the elite were wealthy tenant farmers who, although they did not own land, had sufficient livestock and capital to rent and operate one or more large estates. Some of them had working capital that included a hundred or more yoke of oxen, with their plows and other equipment.[13] They were typical of the south, and in Andalusia they were known, and their modern equivalents still are known, as *labradores*, a term that elsewhere meant a well-to-do peasant with a yoke of animals.[14] They were the counterpart of the large tenant farmers in eighteenth-century England, or the *fermiers généraux* in France.

Contemporaries referred to all these people, both lay and ecclesiastical, legal owners or not, who drew large incomes from the soil and lorded it over their inferiors as the *poderosos*, the powerful ones. It was a term frequent in southern Spain but also used in the north, the eighteenth-century equivalent of "landed elite."[15]

A hundred and fifty years later, between 1906 and 1930, the monarchy carried out a new cadastral survey of central and southern Spain. This became the basis for various studies made during the Second Republic. Recently Edward Malefakis has reviewed all this material and also more sketchy information compiled for the rest of Spain by the Franco regime. His analysis forms the first part of his book *Agrarian Reform and Peasant Revolution in Spain*. He shows that large properties were still concentrated in south and southwest Spain. In this region holdings of over 250 hectares made up 41 percent of the area and accounted for 28 percent of the taxable land value, whereas in the center and east of Spain the corresponding figures were 16 and 6 percent, and in the north and northeast only 8 and 5 percent.[16] The largest proprietors belonged to the titled aristocracy: in the six major provinces of the southern region 176 titled families owned estates of more than 500 hectares (21 of them of more than 5000 hectares), and of these families 124 (70 percent) held titles granted before 1800. Malefakis corroborates our previous evidence that aristocrats who received their titles in the nineteenth century on the average did not acquire such extensive estates as their predecessors had. Alongside these titled aristocrats, however, Malefakis finds a numerically and economically more important group of what he calls "bourgeois" owners.[17] They form the modern equivalent of the eighteenth-century landed hidalgos. The cadastral surveys do not provide information about large tenant farmers, but they also remain a powerful class, as can be seen in the direct observations of Juan Martínez Alier, an economist who has recently looked at Córdoba province.[18] The continuity of patterns from the eighteenth to the twentieth century is thus remarkable. Indeed, the continuity can be pushed back to the period following the reconquest of Spain from the Muslims, when most of the patterns of land distribution first took shape.[19]

Nevertheless, changes had occurred in the nineteenth century, some obvious, others more subtle. The church as an institution and the clergy as a class no longer owned much land, since the government sold off ecclesiastical properties in the nineteenth century.[20] Furthermore, family estates were no longer entailed, the vínculo and mayorazgo having been abolished in 1836.[21] Henceforth, the Spanish law that all direct heirs had to share in the inheritance applied to all classes, although one heir could be favored. Two more subtle changes in the nineteenth century can only be inferred from the evidence available, for we lack long-term comparative studies for specific regions that would confirm them. These are a growth in absenteeism among large owners and increasing intermarriage among them to produce regional family alliances.

From what one can tell, absenteeism is a practice that started at the top of the social and economic scale and worked down. When Napoleon seized the crown of Spain for his brother in 1808, his commander in Madrid furnished him with a list of the Spanish aristocrats living in that capital. It included 60 grandes (half the total number of grandes in 1787).[22] In 1932 the records of the Spanish government show the birthplace of the current 262 grandes, a fair indication of the permanent residence of their parents about the turn of the century. Sixty-eight percent were born in Madrid and 13 percent abroad (5 percent in Paris). Nineteen percent were born elsewhere in Spain, all but 4 percent in major cities.[23] These figures show that insofar as the grandes were landowners, they were mostly absentees, city dwellers, a landed elite by virtue of possession of the land rather than by permanent rural residence. It is possible that their absenteeism had increased since 1808, but one cannot be sure because so many recent grandes were not large landowners.

Absenteeism was less marked among the lower levels of the elite, but here it definitely seems to have been on the increase. In 1808 only

15 percent of the lesser aristocracy lived in Madrid,[24] while the hidalgo owners of Andalusia usually resided in the towns where the majority of their estates were located. In the nineteenth century this pattern changed, to judge from the information collected by Miguel Bernal for Seville province. Agrarian prosperity in the two decades after 1850 encouraged large nonaristocratic owners to move to the cities, where they could engage in politics and educate their sons for liberal professions.[25] Malefakis found that for the early twentieth century absenteeism was still substantially higher among the aristocracy than other classes, but was common among "bourgeois" owners and rose as their properties increased in size. In the countryside around Córdoba, 13.5 percent of the area held by nonaristocrats in parcels of less than 500 hectares was owned by absentees; the rate rose to 32.9 percent for properties of more than 5000 hectares.[26] From such sketchy information we can conclude that there was a trend for owners who could afford to do so to move to the cities. Among aristocrats it had begun well before 1800, and developments of the nineteenth century made it possible for progressively lower strata of landowners to copy them.

Intermarriage seems to have followed a related pattern. The landed elite always intermarried, as one would expect, but eighteenth-century marriage alliances of hidalgo families, in contrast to those of aristocratic families, seem to have been local affairs.[27] In the middle of the nineteenth century, Bernal found that in Morón de la Frontera (Seville province), seven family groups allied by marriage and sharing surnames owned 30 percent of the property. Since that time these groups have become so interrelated by marriage that they form one vast family, closely tied to the high society of Seville.[28] In the early twentieth century, Malefakis found that in Badajoz province (Extremadura) 52 percent of the land owned in blocks of 1,000 or more hectares belonged to twenty-five extended families of more than one sibling group, while only 23 percent belonged to unrelated individuals.[29] Many of the extended families included both titled and non-titled members. Absenteeism and intermarriage were obviously connected, for moving to the city would bring together socially landowners from different parts of a region and encourage family alliances among them. An interlocking landed elite that began under the old regime among the aristocrats was spreading downward to broader layers. How frequently marriage took place between this elite and families of urban origin has not been studied. When it occurred, one would anticipate the absorption of the urban families into the culture and political objectives of the landowners, rather on the English model described by F. M. L. Thompson. Their union formed the cornerstone of the late nineteenth-century Castilian political oligarchy.[30]

The elite that emerges from these studies is primarily a phenomenon of southern Spain. This is so partly because there were more large owners in the south, and partly because government reports and historical studies have concentrated on this area. Some flesh, however, has been provided for the abstract definition proposed earlier. Nevertheless, as will become apparent, there were persons elsewhere whose ownership or control of the land was such that others who made their living from the land were put in a position of dependency on them. Let us continue to think in this wider and more structural fashion rather than simply equate the *latifundistas* of southern Spain with the landed elite as we turn to observe the impact on it of the new forces of the nineteenth century.

The phrase "the new forces of the century" calls to mind the more familiar term "modernization." Unfortunately, modernization has no precise meaning. To economists it may connote industrialization; to political scientists, centralization and bureaucracy and mass politics; to sociologists, the end of a society based on legal orders; and to anthropologists, the adoption of the values of Western culture. Obviously no simple process can be labelled as modernization. A number of scholars have recently questioned whether there is any single path, however broadly defined, from a traditional society to a modern one. E. A. Wrigley, for instance, has argued that, in the case of England, industrialization and modernization were distinct currents that, for a while at least, pulled society in opposite directions.[31] One may go a step further and propose that the different histories of European societies in the nineteenth century may be better understood if we systematically break down the concept of modernization into its distinct manifestations and then observe the order and timing of their appearance in each society.

The case of the Spanish landed elite lends weight to such a proposal. It survived the challenges of the nineteenth century with relative success, and this accomplishment can be explained in large measure as a function of the pattern of modernization south of the Pyrenees. Three different forms of modernization that affected rural elites everywhere provide the key to the explanation: one economic, one political, and one cultural.

Except in Catalonia and, toward the end of the century, the Bilbao region, Spanish economic modernization did not take the form of industrialization. The term can be applied more meaningfully to the introduction of liberal economic policies, and in Spain these significantly modified legal titles to land. As we saw, the eighteenth-century royal reformers were already critical of the practice of entail. Faced by rising population and periodic food shortages in the cities, they wanted to improve the efficiency of farming, and they believed that legal prohibitions on the sale of land kept properties in the hands of neglectful landholders and religious institutions. Not all entailed land was badly exploited, but the law did prevent inefficient or heavily indebted owners from selling their properties and thus transferring them to interested exploiters. In his *Ley agraria* Jovellanos justified the end of entail with economic arguments that echoed Adam Smith. Beginning in 1798 the governments of Spain step by step abolished legal restrictions on the sale or transfer of land. To avoid the ruin of the royal credit in times of war and other crises—under pressure from foreign creditors and frightened by the danger of a fiscal collapse such as brought on the French Revolution—the state appropriated the extensive properties of the church and the municipalities and put them on sale at auction to the highest bidder, taking the proceeds and promising to pay 3 percent interest on the sale price to the former owners.[32] Laws of 1798 and 1836–37 ordered the sale of ecclesiastical properties; in 1855 municipal, crown, and other public properties were added. These lands and buildings were thus left to the play of economic forces. A similar philosophy led to the abolition of entail on family estates in 1836, but the government never confiscated these or ordered their sale. Aristocratic and other mayorazgos were no longer inalienable, but were exposed to the working of the market and to the laws of inheritance, with results that could only be observed over a long period of years. All this legislation produced a profound alteration in property rights. Let us see how it affected the major sectors of the landed elite.

There is very little information on the impact of the end of the mayorazgo. Jaime Vicens Vives believed that it produced a vast transfer of land out of noble hands. He cites the figure of 273,000 properties sold by 1854; but he does not state how this figure was obtained, nor is it clear how it could be, given the nature of the documentary sources.[33] We do know that some distinguished families frittered away their properties. The dukes of Frias spent much of their wealth in support of liberal causes; while the dukes of Medina Sidonia and Osuna had little land left by 1930.[34] The count of Torres Cabrera experimented with the introduction of sugar beets in Córdoba province at the end of the century with disastrous financial results that left him only 600 hectares.[35] On the whole, however, the impact of economic forces does not appear to have been harmful until after the First World War, and not all sales indicated monetary losses. The Medinaceli family sold its estates in Córdoba in the twentieth century to its tenants as a calculated step to transfer capital to urban properties and industry.[36] In any case, one can counterbalance these losses by other gains. The marquis of Comillas, a successful shipping magnate who received his title in 1878, founded a family that by 1932 owned 24,000 hectares, the sixth largest private holding in Spain.[37] Malefakis found in a detailed analysis of parts of four southern provinces that 13 percent of noble landholdings in 1930 had been purchased by the current owner.[38]

Vicens Vives recognizes that on the whole the aristocracy preserved its estates pretty much unscathed. To explain the many sales he records, he suggests that it was the lower nobility that sold out. Raymond Carr, following him, credits the abolition of the mayorazgo with destroying "the secure world of the *hidalgo*."[39] One might explain such a development if as a class the hidalgos had been heavily in debt and were now faced with foreclosures. In the sixteenth and seventeenth centuries many of the high aristocracy obtained permission from the crown to establish oppressive perpetual liens (*censos*) on their mayorazgos.[40] We lack studies, however, on the extent of liens on the thousands of small entails belonging to hidalgos. It is doubtful that they were ever as serious a burden as they were for the aristocracy. In any case, since agriculture was prospering in the nineteenth century, hidalgos should not have had to dispose of their estates to meet inherited obligations. For this reason one would not expect the transfer of property following the end of entail to harm them collectively. Even if there were as many sales as Vicens says, they do not necessarily establish the ruin of a social class. Many mayorazgos had properties scattered across the country, with resulting high costs of administration and little supervision. The end of entail gave owners the possibility of selling some properties and buying others with the objective of rationalizing their overall exploitation. The time was especially opportune, since ecclesiastical and municipal lands were being auctioned off by the government. Furthermore, Vicens' figures indicate that only a small proportion of noble property was exchanged. He gives the value of those sold as one billion reales; by 1856 the forced sale of church properties had brought in six times this amount, yet nobles originally owned more land than the church.[41] The most significant effect of the law was not that it ruined a gentry class but that it prodded that class toward efficient management and improvement as the condition for remaining well-to-do.

Very different was the working of the forced sales of church and municipal properties, for these produced a vast exchange in the ownership of agricultural land. I have estimated that between one-quarter and one-third of all property, measured by its value rather than its area, was sold in this way.[42] The term *desamortización* that applies to these sales is infamous in modern Spanish history. Its critics have popularized two views of desamortización: that it produced a bourgeois revolution in the countryside and that it subverted a needed agrarian reform that would distribute land to poor peasants and farm workers. Both of these views are wrong in my estimation, although only the first one calls for extensive discussion here. Desamortización did not change the basic structure of landholding: minifundia remained typical of the center and north and latifundia of the south.[43] This result was to be expected, for church properties, which were the majority of those sold, were a fair cross section of local properties. Their transfer to new owners would not alter the pattern of relative size of holdings. On the contrary, the working of economic laws would accentuate local characteristics. The sale of lands at auction enabled the more wealthy bidders to get the properties. Where property and wealth were already concentrated, sales would add to concentration. Where properties were small and wealth widely distributed, as in hilly and mountainous regions, purchases would be diffused and more equal.[44]

Near Salamanca, where ecclesiastical institutions owned many small plots of land, the forced sale of these holdings permitted wealthy individuals of the city to buy up blocks of fields which they then rented out to peasants as the church had done before. In the period 1798–1808, the extreme case was Don Francisco Alonso Moral, a grain merchant and administrator of various large estates, who bought about five hundred fields and meadows in at least twenty-four towns.[45] When he was finished, he had as many tenant farmers as a wealthy religious house. He was but the largest of a number of buyers, who included notaries, university professors, beneficed clergy, royal officials, administrators, landowners, merchants, and a military officer. Such transfers show that a lay landed elite could develop in those areas of central and northern Spain where there were no large estates without changing fundamentally the pattern of property holding. Studies of Álava (Basque provinces) and Gerona (Catalonia) later in the century indicate the emergence of similar owners of many small properties there.[46]

In these and other areas wealthy urban residents replaced urban ecclesiastical institutions as the holders of rural property. This development has been put forward as proof of a bourgeois revolution in landholding. The conclusion rests on the usually unstated assumption that all men of wealth who did not have titles were bourgeois, but the assumption can be very misleading. We have seen how mixed was the group of large Salamanca buyers at the beginning of the century. In Baños (Jaén) the hidalgo families who dominated the town in the eighteenth century were among those that bought the most land in the first disentail of 1798. Shall we call them bourgeois because they had no titles? Even the fact that the buyers of the mid-nineteenth century lived in cities is no proof that they were previously alien to landowning, for we have seen that landed families were moving to the cities.[47]

Simple reason would suggest that just as the working of the sales at auction preserved local land distribution, so did it preserve local social structures—minus, of course, the clergy as a separate landed class. Outside Catalonia—and Madrid and a few other large cities—a strong bourgeois class, whether eager for land or not, was hardly present. Auction gave the advantage to those with money, and in agricultural regions these were mainly the people who directly or indirectly drew their wealth from the land. Not all owned land before, but throughout most of Spain they all formed part of a social structure long geared to agriculture as the final source of income. Salamanca, a university city and ecclesiastical and administrative center, was not typical. Yet even here large buyers in the first disentail included all types of men of wealth, many of them receiving their income more or less directly from the agricultural economy. As the century progressed the really large properties everywhere often went to distant men of wealth, especially in Madrid, some of them speculators, some merchants, some government officials, and some also landowners.[48] Except in the industrial cities and perhaps Madrid, however, one suspects that the landed elite soon absorbed socially and culturally those outsiders who bought large holdings.

Some writers have recognized that the buyers were largely made up of landowners, but nevertheless cannot abandon the idea that the desamortización effected a bourgeois revolution. For them the adoption of a classical free economy, based on alienable private property, wage labor, and production for the market, involves the triumph of a bourgeois class. Even if its members were not previously bourgeois, this interpretation asserts that their new relationship to land, labor, and capital now made them so.[49] As if nobles had not hired labor and sought profits under the old regime! When one looks at the process without a preconceived expectation of finding a bourgeois revolution, one sees that the landed elite that took shape was an amalgam of new and old elements, and not properly speaking bourgeois, either culturally or economically.

By a strange mingling of conceptions, the same writers who find an aggressive bourgeoisie taking advantage of the desamortización to seize control of the land frequently describe the new owners as an idle, spendthrift, leisure class. Francisco Simón Segura, the leading Spanish student of the desamortización, describes the new owner: "The capitalist born of the desamortización did not pursue the maximum profit with the intention of reinvesting it rapidly and thus increasing the social product, he did not place himself in the service of society. Rather, a devotee of elegant living, of the daily gathering in the cafe, of hunting, he did not venture risk capital in his affairs, and thus he lacked the fundamental feature of the entrepreneurial spirit."[50] Simón and others judge desamortización an economic failure, wasting Spain's accumulated capital in a vain search for status. In their view, since savings were exhausted in the purchase of land, the new owners lacked capital for improvement and modernization of agriculture, or to invest in industry. Again I think reality is hidden by popular misconceptions, no doubt inspired by the example of real individuals but exaggerated by reformers and critics of the landowning class. The early nineteenth century saw a vast breaking of pasture and marginal lands for planting grain. After 1860, when grain was no longer so profitable, olive groves and vines replaced wheat over wide areas.[51] All these changes represented capital investment in production for a national and international market, and many of the larger owners and beneficiaries of land sales must have been in the forefront of the movement. When the revolution of 1868 led to a law for the auction of mineral rights in Spain, foreign investors obtained the richest mines. In this area Spaniards with capital had little experience or economic commitment. But Spaniards kept control of their best agricultural land, although foreigners were free to buy, and products of the soil rivalled minerals as leading exports at the end of the century.[52] The growth of commercial agriculture favored the rise of merchants and others involved in this trade with profits which they could in turn use to buy land. Wealth could spread out from agriculture and return in this way. The end of the entailed family mayorazgo facilitated the success of the more enterprising agricultural entrepreneurs. The critics of the desamortización believe a distribution of land to small peasants would have been more just and beneficial, but the economics of the situation suggest that such a policy would have retarded Spain's agricultural progress and in the long run would not have benefited even the peasantry.[53]

On the whole desamortización was carried out in a fashion that would strengthen the landowning class and others familiar with agriculture. It helped the strong and aggressive to get stronger; in economic terms by freeing the factors of production from legal restrictions it favored those who used them most efficiently. What the Spanish case shows is that the growth of a mercantile, industrial class is not a prerequisite for the adoption of laissez faire policies. In an agricultural country, enterprising men engaged in exploiting the land and in marketing its products stood to benefit from freeing the market in real property in a time of rising demand for agricultural goods. Here economic modernization was not alien to a landed elite, but rather gave new life to an old social structure, minus, of course, its clerical sector.

Political modernization would be a different matter. Spain's change from the absolute monarchy of the old regime to parliamentary government—permanently so after 1834—and eventually to universal suffrage in 1890; the abolition of seigneurial jurisdictions in 1836; and the growing power of the centralized state all represented obvious attacks on the power of a landed oligarchy, although the clergy and the monarchy were more direct victims. By their very nature, the workings of classical economics and political democracy were bound to conflict. The former enabled those in control of capital and land to advance at the expense of the less capable and less fortunate majority, while prohibiting workers from associating to present a united front against their superiors. Political democracy, in theory at least, measured power not by wealth but by individual votes. It legitimized the cooperation of the many through the electoral and legislative process to curb the power of the few, and through majority action to restore an economic balance. With reason the ruling classes of nineteenth-century Europe feared that universal suffrage would attack property rights—the cornerstone of classical economics—and introduce socialism.

Yet the Spanish landed elite managed to stave off the threat. The abolition of seigneurial jurisdictions does not appear to have had much effect on the real situation. Seigneurial rights were less profitable in most parts of Spain than in France and had not been the basis for a feudal reaction. Señores with jurisdiction were mostly titled aristocrats, and we have seen that they did not fare badly. Salvador de Moxó, the leading student of the end of the señoríos, argues that on the contrary, señores seized the opportunity to turn their jurisdictions into private property, converting feudal dues into rents.[54] I cannot believe that this was a widespread achievement. The census of 1787 shows that about half the towns and villages in Spain were under lay seigneurial jurisdiction; obviously no substantial proportion of them ever became the outright property of former señores.

The establishment of parliamentary government and universal suffrage was a much more direct threat. The landed elite responded in a curious way. In the eighteenth century its political power rested on its control of local government. Señores made appointments to local offices in their señoríos, while wealthy hidalgo families in the south owned municipal offices and often made appointments to local ecclesiastical benefices as well. Meanwhile, with the advent of the Bourbons, the royal government had come into the hands of councillors and bureaucrats who thought primarily in terms of national economic and military needs. Among their projects, they tried to distribute municipal lands to independent peasant farmers, in the process threatening the economic power of the elite. They failed because municipal governments did not carry out their decrees, and the royal bureaucracy was too rudimentary to do the job.[55]

In the nineteenth century a peculiar thing happened. To effect reform, beginning with the Constitution of 1812, the liberals sought to make municipal offices elective. When in power, the conservatives responded by requiring that mayors (*alcaldes*) be appointees of the central government and its provincial agents. The reason is that once royal absolutism was replaced by parliamentary government, the elites of the country, including the ubiquitous landed elite, discovered that their power was better guaranteed by controlling the central authority than by resisting it locally. In the process they developed the institution known as *caciquismo*, a word more infamous in recent Spanish history even than desamortización.

As it is usually understood, caciquismo was a form of political bossism, whereby the bosses or *caciques* preserved themselves and their associates in political control of the country by violating the legal constitutional order. The term *cacique* was used already in the eighteenth century to describe the man with most local power,[56] but its application to political bosses became common about 1880.[57] It replaced the old regime term *poderoso*, but it did not represent simply a new word for the rural oligarchs; a new function was involved. Much was written at the turn of the century on caciquismo—most famous was Joaquín Costa's memoir on the subject for the Ateneo de Madrid and the responses to his request for comments by leading Spaniards[58] —and much is being written now.[59] After the defeat of 1898, Spanish reformers found in caciquismo the epitome of what was wrong with Spain. For them it was proof that the country was backward, uncivilized, and divorced from contemporary progress in western Europe. Costa hoped for a "surgeon of iron" to excise this cancer.

The classic picture of caciquismo is given life by the description by one of Costa's respondents of an electoral district in Córdoba province:

> For more than a quarter of a century these patient Andalusians support a cacique regime which, though typical, has its peculiar features. The district is the fief—in appearance alternating but in fact simultaneous—of two former judges of the Supreme Court, one of them a Conservative, the other a Liberal Unionist, and brothers-in-law to each other. Their brother-in-law-hood is so effusive that word has gone down to both bands that in all political and administrative statements the clients of one band are to refer to their counterparts in the other as their brothers-in-law. Both bands recognize the immediate command of a certain Don Bartolomé Tolico, the ambidextrous steward of the Liberal and Conservative leaders. When the Conservatives are in power, Tolico is cacique as delegate of Don A.; when the Liberals take their place, Tolico hurls thunderbolts and issues ukases as plenipotentiary of Don B. His empire is so absolute that the entire life of the district depends on him. When a drought scorches the fields, the local people say, "Tolico does not want it to rain." I do not have to explain that throughout the width and breadth of the fief, mayors, judges, and priests, with a possible rare exception, are perpetually Tolicated.[60]

The original critics of caciquismo saw it essentially as a response to parliamentary government, an instrument created to manipulate the system so that the free wishes of the public would not become known or obeyed. For them, its primary function was to arrange elections in order to maintain in power the two established parties of the end of the century, the Conservatives of Cánovas and the Liberals of Sagasta, alternating peacefully in control of the ministry. On the surface, Spain politically mirrored England; beneath the surface, it was run by and for the caciques and their associates. Since Costa's day much ink has flowed in describing how the caciques managed elections. While electoral corruption emerges conclusively, who the caciques were does not. Caciquismo seems easier to get hold of than the cacique himself. Was he the local party leader? Was he the local economic potentate? Was he an upstart and unscrupulous civil servant? All these characterizations have been applied, yet none describes him satisfactorily or explains his power.

The reason, I think, is that both since and before Costa the critics of caciquismo have misunderstood its nature. They have believed that it was the result of the malfunctioning of the political system and that its cure lay in political reform. What had occurred, if my analysis is correct, is that the collapse of the old regime after the Napoleonic invasion brought with it a collapse of the royal bureaucracy. The alternating governments of the nineteenth century tried to revive the bureaucracy and rationalize it, while extending its functions down to local affairs as was occurring elsewhere in western Europe. They succeeded in creating both administrative and judicial hierarchies, but the legitimacy and authority of these were weakened by frequent civil strife and revolutions. With the establishment of parliamentary government a second kind of hierarchic network also developed, the organized political party. As elsewhere, the political party as a permanent organization took time to emerge. The Moderados were the first to create one, under Isabel II, with the purpose of influencing elections.[61] It evolved into the late nineteenth-century Conservative party, and others followed, mostly to the left of it. Yet neither the state administrative and judicial hierarchies nor the political parties offered a reliable instrument for the elites to use in keeping the country running as they wished. Political parties alternated in power, state bureaucrats varied with revolutions and restorations. Thus a third parallel hierarchy of authority and administration arose that had no constitutional or legal role but became the effective network for enforcing the policies of those with social and economic power. Although not all its members were labelled caciques, we may call it the cacique hierarchy. Unlike the other hierarchies, its personnel remained relatively permanent and fixed in their geographic localities.[62]

Since it had no legal or constitutional basis, the cacique network was held together from top to bottom by private contacts and personal loyalty, cemented by self-interest. The feature of direct personal association led contemporaries, when they sought comparisons for caciquismo, to liken it to feudalism and thereby demonstrate Spain's backwardness.[63] It had a certain similarity to a lord-vassal system, for the typical cacique appeared to have authority over a private fief, was responsible to a higher cacique, and had others under him. It differed, however, in at least two major ways from feudalism. First, it was extra-legal and therefore fulfilled functions which by law belonged to constituted authorities, and second, its members did not belong to a single recognized social or legal class. One finds identified as caciques national and local party leaders, secretaries of municipal councils, powerful landowners, hidalgos, doctors, lawyers, merchants, even small shopkeepers.[64]

The critics of caciquismo have tried to establish a functional connection between the public role of caciques and their membership in the cacique hierarchy, but the resulting explanations run into serious difficulties. Seeing them as the local heads of the political parties leads to such improbable assertions as that local party leaders were prepared to support their political rivals in elections in order to preserve the system, or that both parties employed the same local cacique. Neither can the cacique network be understood as having a direct relationship with the administrative organization of the state. One contemporary shook his head at the problem posed for anyone trying to govern the country through such a maze: in provinces where a known man was cacique the task was easy, but what to do "in those happy provinces where a head of a bureau rules in three towns, a director has a district and a half, and a subsecretary has two parts of an electoral district"?[65] I believe that the mistaken identification of caciques with political henchmen or office holders has arisen because membership in the three hierarchies, state, party, and cacique, frequently overlapped. Both local party leaders and local civil servants could belong to the cacique network, but they fulfilled functions of that network in their role as caciques and not those of their public positions.

Since the purpose of this network was to effect privately determined policies, it had to subvert the official hierarchies, in so far as these stood for impartial administration and law enforcement. While corrupting elections was the most famous achievement of caciques, their day to day activity was to see that local administrators and judges carried out policies determined by those to whom the cacique network was subservient rather than the policies that law and equity prescribed. Large owners paid ridiculously low property taxes, judges rendered biased decisions, administrators granted favors, made arrests, and in general enforced the law selectively all according to the instructions of the relevant cacique. There was no question where authority lay. The highest official in the province was the civil governor yet the president of the association of ex-governors stated bitterly: "In the struggles between governors and caciques, the governors are usually right; but since the caciques are immovable, the governors have to leave."[66] Reforming administrators found themselves transferred, and honest judges stagnated in courts of the first instance while those who cooperated rose in the system.[67] An astute observer noted that caciquismo had separated appointments of local officials from the central government just as señorios and the purchase of municipal office had done under the old regime.[68] And yet it was not a new feudalism, for it was *sub rosa*, acknowledged by no body of recognized law.

Neither was it a form of patron-client relationship, as some have
held, although this explanation would be consonant with its extra-legal
existence. It seems virtually impossible to document the nature of
relationships within the hierarchy. Some no doubt were of the nature
of patron and client, but not all. The functions of the network placed
many individuals in a superior-inferior relationship independent of
their personal connections. They cooperated loyally because of more
than personal favors. The astute observer cited above argued that a
cure for caciquismo would be to establish a proper system of *com-
padrazgo* or clientage.[69]

A final comparison that comes to mind is between caciquismo and
the revolutionary political party, like the Jacobins or Nazis, that trans-
mits authority outside the state hierarchy and enforces its policies on
local officials. But caciquismo was not revolutionary, and it was not a
political party. It had no membership lists, no official titles, no publica-
tions. Above all it was not held together by an ideology, for as we
shall see it depended on mass apathy, not political mobilization. One
begins to understand why historians have had such difficulty in pin-
ning it down, and why the present analysis may also turn out to be
incorrect, or only partially correct.

Nothing in the analysis so far has demonstrated that caciquismo was
the institution used by the rural elite to cope with parliamentary
democracy. Many writers have recognized that caciques were often
figureheads, *testaferros*, who served others who hid behind them, the
real oligarchs. Costa entitled his report *Oligarchy and Caciquismo as
the Present Form of the Government of Spain*. One of his respondents
described the cacique as "the representative of an oligarch who exercises unlimited public functions without legal authority in a province,
district, or municipality by means of the legitimately established
authorities, who have been placed under his orders by the person
who appointed them. The power of the cacique derives from the
influence that the oligarch he represents has with the central government."[70] While contemporaries described the caciques in detail, they
did not seek the structure of the oligarchy behind them. Most seem to
have been too convinced that the problem was primarily political or
administrative to have sought an explanation in the social or economic
structure of the country.

We may approach the problem indirectly. To see whose interests
caciquismo served, we can ask who did not need it. The answer is the
vast majority of people, who would have been better off if the law had
been fairly and strictly applied and if freely chosen delegates had
enacted legislation in their interest. Since a democratic parliamentary

system aimed to favor the majority, the logical reason for the existence of caciquismo was to protect those whom democracy could
hurt. The reasoning outlined above points to those whom the liberal
economic system favored, the powerful economic interests, the upper
classes, the elites. This rather obvious conclusion is not new. The
historian Joaquín Romero Maura has explained: "In the zones of the
country where powerful economic interests organized themselves as
pressure groups, the local caciques—when they did not achieve their
position through the help of these groups—placed themselves at their
head or tried by all means to cooperate in their victory." He sees them
working for textile manufacturers in Catalonia, mining interests in
Asturias, and wheat growers in Castile.[71] Reality was much less simple
than this, however, or the point would have been made long ago.
Caciques obtained favorable administrative decisions for modest citizens, they got local youths exempted from the draft, had local taxes
reduced across the board, and in other ways seemed at times to be
benevolent despots. Here they did act in the role of patron. But they
also served the acquired interests, local cliques, the political parties,
and not least the other persons in the cacique network. Caciquismo
was not more prevalent in regions of large properties like Andalusia
than in those of small peasant farms. Various writers point to Asturias,
a province of minifundia in the north, as suffering from deeply entrenched caciquismo.[72] It will help us to conceive of caciquismo as an
instrument of the rural elite (among other elites), if we keep to our
general definition of that elite rather than substitute for it only the
southern latifundistas.

In the present state of our knowledge it is hard to see how the
wishes of the elites became the commands of the cacique network.
One suggestion is that the ministry contained the heads of both the
cacique and the political networks, and that it represented the major
national interests.[73] This is undoubtedly true, for the parliamentary
monarchy established by the Moderados in the middle of the century
worked to reconcile the various national and foreign interests in Spain.
Fortunately for them the various interests tended to be strong in
different geographical regions. Where they conflicted, the ministerial
system usually could work out a compromise; and if they seriously fell
out, the threat or fact of revolution served to bring them back together.[74] But unity of interests among persons at the highest level,
while undoubtedly critical, cannot be a complete explanation. There
must have been a myriad of ways operating tangentially up and down
the hierarchy whereby oligarchies worked as groups and impressed
their will on caciques. So far as the landed elite is concerned, we recall

that it was moving into the cities and becoming more and more inter-married on a regional level. One result is that it would become a series of much more consciously integrated oligarchic groups and another is that it would need agents, straw men, caciques, in the smaller towns and countryside to enforce its will. The term *cacique* replaced *poderoso* because the poderosos were disappearing from the scene leaving the caciques to fend for them.

Two examples of the many described by Costa's respondents show how caciquismo drew a veil over the naked power of the large land-owners. The first involves a Spanish corporation established to build a dam and exploit mineral resources in southern Spain, activities that roused landowners' apprehensions, especially because they introduced industrial conflicts. The corporation carefully appointed to its govern-ing board some associates of the local cacique. The undertaking started propitiously enough, but soon it began to feel a hostile atmosphere. Its projects were delayed and official authorizations failed to come through. The anonymous author of the account we have, a member of the governing board, offered personally to catch the cacique and give him a thrashing, convinced that all the local inhabitants would come out of hiding to applaud. The others were more circumspect. The president explained: "An ill-humored frown of the señor would be enough for ninety percent of the local landowners to deny us permis-sion to build our aerial tramway over their fields. A nod from him will open up private properties and obtain the licenses of municipal coun-cils. One must recognize the facts. What are we to do? Live in peace and submission to the cacique, seek his friendship, and solicit his pro-tection." The author, furious, resigned from the board, telling them they were acting like women. "And everyone knows," he said, "what happens to women sooner or later, by the law of nature." The cor-poration sought to avoid this fate by a more subtle defense. It named a foreign citizen to the governing board.[75]

The second illustration comes from the letter of a judge of the first instance:

> I recall, among other examples, the case of a poor farm laborer, brought to court for the misdemeanor of crossing an open field which belonged to an important person of high position in the town. The real purpose was to use this indirect and expeditious means to close a public path across his property. An associate of the cacique, a most devout but un-scrupulous lawyer, argued the case for the plaintiff, and the poor de-fenseless man was convicted in the municipal court. He appealed and obtained a reversal of the verdict, and this judgment led to the circulation of atrocious reports about the judge of the first instance. The plaintiff

pretended to drop the case, but the municipal attorney took it to the Supreme Court. How bad his case was can be judged from the refusal of that court even to consider it.[76]

Costa's respondent makes it clear that the happy ending was not typical, but he is careful not to say where this incident occurred. While it could have taken place anywhere, the refusal of the laborer to be cowed by the local court suggests that it was in a region of independent peasantry, outside southern Spain.

Such was the mechanism by which the landed and other elites maintained local authority and thwarted the democratic challenge. Caciquismo became their primary defense against political modernization, however, only because Spain offered special conditions that derive from the nature of its cultural modernization. Elsewhere—in England, in Germany—conservative forces resorted to ideological appeals to win the support of the common people. They used nationalism and the race for empire to win the masses from the proponents of radical change. In Spain on the contrary, the elites survived thanks to the slowness with which political awareness spread to the bulk of the people. Ideological commitment is one aspect of the third kind of modernization which affected nineteenth-century landowning classes: the development among the people of awareness of, and participation in, new cultural phenomena. Since acceptance of new ideologies is one of these phenomena, cultural modernization joins hands with political modernization, but they are not identical. Cultural modernization is a function of such forces as urbanization, universal education, and the growth of communications. In this area Spain differed much more from northern Europe than in its economic and political institutions.

Elsewhere I have tried to explain the political history of nineteenth-century Spain by reference to the anthropologist Robert Redfield's division of the culture of a preindustrial society into a "great tradition," the rational written culture of the educated classes who hold the levers of power, and the "little tradition" of the unlettered people of the villages.[77] The little tradition follows the great tradition at a distance, adopting its thought patterns crudely and unreflectingly. This is an oversimplified explanation of a complex process, but it conveys the essence. Now, it appears to me that the great tradition in Spain bifurcated in the eighteenth century when a new secular ideology devoted to progress broke with the older authoritarian religious ideology. The bearers of these two ideologies in the nineteenth and twentieth cen-

turies have been called the "two Spains." Slowly the little tradition
also became divided in the same way, as some of those who lived at
this cultural level began to listen to the new great tradition. Proximity
to and communication with the bearers of the new ideology were
critical, for I would go beyond Redfield and apply the term little
tradition to lower class urban culture as well as village culture. The
urban lower classes, witnesses to the political involvement of their
employers and to revolutionary municipal juntas and exposed to the
press, speeches, and other political propaganda, became politicized and
adopted crude versions of the new tradition, the catchwords of re-
publicanism, anarchism, and socialism. After the revolutions of mid-
century, spawned in the cities, the Spanish elites, unlike most of their
European counterparts, made no concerted effort to direct an ideological appeal to this audience.

The rural lower classes remained cut off from modern thought patterns. The railroad network was skimpy, and there were few decent
roads. Most peasants went to the cities rarely, if ever, and felt awk-
ward when they did. They felt alien to the modern world burgeoning
there, and a fortiori to the newfangled parliamentary system. Romero
Maura has denied such ideological isolation of rural Spain, pointing to
the many peasant youths who gained experience in the armies that
fought in nineteenth-century civil wars, and to the millions who went
to America to work and returned.[78] He also points to the local priests
as a channel for contact with modern culture, but here I think is
rather one of the keys of the continued rural isolation from modern
ideologies. Because liberals and republicans had destroyed his traditional way of life and the basis of his income, the priest painted the
new great tradition as evil and helped keep the peasants loyal to the
old great tradition. If local civil servants reflected the will of the
caciques, their presence would have a similar effect. Most villagers did
not want to vote, or to defend their civil rights, or to challenge the
legality of the caciques' actions, because to do so was alien to their
concept of what society expected or would tolerate. Caciquismo flourished on their ignorance, apathy, and lack of awareness of national
issues, on a "ruralization" of political life, as one author called it.[79]

While contemporary critics did not as a rule seek to explain caciquismo through a study of the ruling elites, the more perceptive were
well aware that cultural backwardness made it possible. Besides his
"surgeon of iron," Costa saw the need for long-term medication: education and economic betterment of the common people were the cures
he prescribed.[80] Popular education, the creation of an enlightened
public ready for a constitutional system, the raising of the Spanish

people to the level of the rest of Europe, were the recommendations of the philosopher Miguel de Unamuno, the scientist Santiago Ramón y Cajal, and the novelist Emilia Pardo Bazán.[81]

It would appear that Spain's slow progress in cultural modernization can be explained to a great extent by the fact that its economic modernization was largely agricultural and rural rather than industrial and urban. In turn, cultural backwardness permitted the beneficiaries of economic evolution to subvert the parliamentary system. This peculiar syncopation in the different manifestations of modernization gave Spain unique characteristics. One of the earliest countries in Europe to become permanently parliamentary, it was one of the slowest in adopting mass political parties.

Cultural modernization could be checked only so long. By the end of the nineteenth century, it was growing apace. Catalan manufacturers appealed to Catalan nationalism to build up a following against Madrid and against their own workers, and in the process they destroyed caciquismo in their region.[82] More critical for the landed elite was the appearance of anarchism in Andalusia in the last third of the century. It arose where agricultural workers lived in semi-urban agglomerations and where, as a result, they associated with an urban lower class of craftsmen and small shopkeepers. Even if not industrial, the southern urban setting provided the cultural development needed for a rudimentary mass ideological movement.[83]

Gradually the twentieth century destroyed the conditions whereby the landed elite asserted itself. Industry and cities grew, swinging the balance of power away from agriculture and the countryside. Socialists and anarchists effectively politicized the southern rural workers by the time of the Second Republic. After five years of turmoil, the landed elite was justifiably frightened in the spring of 1936. Rural alienation remained, however, in the center and the north, the regions of small towns, and these areas supported Franco's "crusade." The Franco era has completed the transformation. Increasing industrialization, emigration from the countryside, highway transportation, and television are bringing the rural and urban worlds culturally together throughout the country.

The landed elite has survived, however. Political authoritarianism has replaced caciquismo to fend off the dangers of democracy. Some members of the elite have become modern entrepreneurial agriculturalists, others have diversified their operations to include investment in banking and industry, while others have continued to accumulate lands.[84] In the nineteenth century the landowning class grew stronger and incorporated new members through the process of desamortización, and its old and new members became integrated by associating together in the cities and intermarrying. Now, as agriculture has lost its preponderant position in the economy, they are reinforcing their connections with other leading sectors. The landed elite inherited from the old regime the advantage of control of Spain's main factor of production, but it has survived by its ability to adapt to changing conditions.

NOTES

1. Richard Herr, *The Eighteenth-Century Revolution in Spain* (Princeton, 1958), p. 96.
2. Jaime Vicens Vives et al., *Historia de España y América* (Barcelona, 1961), vol. 5, p. 136.
3. *Guía oficial de España, 1896* (Madrid, 1896), pp. 236–311.
4. Edward E. Malefakis, *Agrarian Reform and Peasant Revolution in Spain: Origins of the Civil War* (New Haven, 1970), pp. 205–19.
5. *Boletín del Instituto de Reforma Agraria*, year 3, no. 25 (July 1934), pp. 539–43; Malefakis, *Agrarian Reform*, pp. 222–24.
6. The Marquis of Comillas, the great shipping magnate, was the only grande whose original title was granted in the nineteenth century to have over 10,000 hectares of expropriable property. Thirteen families with titles going back before 1800 did. (Calculated on the basis of sources cited in notes 3 and 5; see also Malefakis, *Agrarian Reform*, table 17, p. 71.)
7. Miguel Bernal is engaged in an extensive investigation of landowning in Seville province in the nineteenth century, but most of the results are still unpublished. The following have appeared: A.-M. Bernal, "Formación y desarrollo de la burguesía agraria sevillana: caso concreto de morón de la Frontera," *La question de la "bourgeoisie" dans le monde hispanique au XIX⁰ siècle: Colloque international organisé par l'Institut d'Etudes Ibériques et Ibéro-américaines de l'Université de Bordeaux III en février 1970* (Bibliothèque de l'Ecole des Hautes Etudes Hispaniques, fascicule 45: Bordeaux, 1973), pp. 47–69; Miguel Bernal, "Le minifundium dans le régime latifundiaire d'Andalusie," *Mélanges de la Casa de Velasquez*, 7 (1972): 379–406. Both are reprinted in Antonio Miguel Bernal, *La propiedad de la tierra y las luchas agrarias andaluzas* (Barcelona, 1974). See also n. 30 below.
8. See Pierre Vilar, "*Motín de Esquilache* et crises d'ancien régime," in *Historia ibérica*, no. 1, *Economía y sociedad en los siglos XVIII y XIX* (New York, 1973), pp. 11–33; Pierre Vilar, "El 'Motín de Esquilache,'" *Revista de Occidente*, no. 107 (Feb. 1972), pp. 199–249; Laura Rodriguez, "The Spanish Riots of 1766," *Past & Present*, no. 59 (May 1973), pp. 119–46.
9. Gonzalo Anes Alvarez, "El Informe sobre la Ley Agraria y la Real Sociedad Económica Matritense de Amigos del País," in *Homenaje a Don Ramón Carande* (Madrid, 1963), 1:23–56, republished in Gonzalo Anes Álvarez, *Economía e 'Ilustración' en la España del siglo XVIII* (Madrid, 1969), pp. 95–138.
10. The best available estimate of eighteenth-century ecclesiastical property, based on the totals of the cadastral survey for the provinces of Castile, is provided in Richard Herr, "Hacia el derrumbe del Antiguo Régimen: crisis fiscal y desamortización bajo Carlos IV," *Moneda y Crédito*, no. 118 (Sept. 1971), pp. 37–

100, tables 2 and 3 (income of ecclesiastical property in Castile: 236.6 million reales; of all property: 1,248.0 million reales). We lack firm figures on noble holdings at the end of the Old Regime, since the cadastre did not distinguish between noble and nonnoble lay owners. Alexandre Moreau de Jonnès, *Statistique de l'Espagne* (Paris, 1834), p. 127, quotes Charles III's adviser Francisco de Cabarrús as providing the following figures for all Spain:

	Area millions of hectares	Net Income* millions of francs (1 franc = 4 reales)
32,279 ecclesiastical establishments	1.38	19.32
1,323 noble families	16.94	237.16
396,034 hidalgos and bourgeois	9.16	128.24
vacant land	9.82	

*including buildings and livestock

Such figures can only have been informed guesses, since the cadastre, the only full survey, was not totaled for area but only for income and did not cover the crown of Aragon. The income stated for ecclesiastical properties is far below that of the cadastre, and this inconsistency casts doubt on the validity of the table as a whole.

Raymond Carr, *Spain, 1808–1939* (Oxford, 1966), p. 39, n. 1, says: "A very rough estimate of the distribution of landed property in Spain *c.* 1800 is: Church 9.09 million *fanegas*; Nobility 28.3; Commoners 17.5 (the *fanega* = 0.64 hectares)." These figures come originally from a table given to the Cortes of Cadiz in 1811 by a deputy who favored the abolition of seigneurial jurisdictions. They refer to the types of jurisdiction in which lands were located, and not to the ownership of property. The specification was cultivated lands given over to grains and vegetables, excluding waste and pasture land (*baldíos y montes*), that were under royal jurisdiction (*realenga*), lay seigneurial jurisdiction (*señorios seculares*), and ecclesiastical jurisdiction, including that of the military orders (*señorios eclesiásticos y órdenes militares*). The figures are of *aranzadas* (the aranzada was 0.45 hectares). He gave no source. (Alonso y Lopez, 27 June 1811, *Diario de las Cortes*, v. 6, pp. 475–76). The economist José Canga Argüelles picked up this table but changed its meaning. He entitled it "The cultivated lands that exist in Spain, according to the class of owners to whom they belong." Lands under royal jurisdiction he called of *manos vivas* (belonging to owners who did not have their lands in entail), and the others of *señores* and *manos muertas* (under ecclesiastical entail). (José Canga Argüelles, *Diccionario de hacienda con aplicación a España* [Madrid, 1834], s.v. "Tierras cultivadas que hay en España con distincion de clase de los poseedores a que pertenecen.") Presumably, Carr got his figures from Canga Argüelles, changing aranzadas to fanegas.

In the present state of our knowledge, we really have no reliable figures for titled, noble, or entailed estates in the old regime. The most extravagant claim for the nobility, clearly wrong although often cited, is by Vicens Vives that in 1500 the nobles possessed 97 percent of the surface of the peninsula, either as direct property or under seigneurial jurisdiction. Of this, he says, 45 percent belonged to the church. (Jaime Vicens Vives, *An Economic History of Spain*, trans. Frances Lopez-Morillas [Princeton, 1969], p. 295.)

11. Archivo Histórico Provincial de Jaén: Catastro de la Ensenada, única contribución, libros 62–66.

12. This information is based on a study of *desamortización* under Charles IV that I am currently working on. See Richard Herr, "La vente des propriétés de

mainmorte en Espagne, 1798–1808," *Annales: Économies, Sociétés, Civilisations*, 29 (1974): 215–28.

13. *Memorial ajustado hecho de orden del Consejo . . . sobre los daños, y decadencia que padece la Agricultura . . .* (Madrid, 1784), para. 660. This memorial was republished, slightly abridged, in "El espediente de reforma agraria en el siglo XVIII," ed. Antonio Elorza, *Revista de Trabajo*, no. 17 (1967), pp. 138–310. The paragraphs are numbered the same, and my references will be to them.

14. *Memorial ajustado*, paras. 658–84; Juan Martínez-Alier, *Labourers and Landowners in Southern Spain* (London, 1971), p. 294, for current practice.

15. *Memorial ajustado*, paras. 133, 248, 294, 661.

16. Malefakis, *Agrarian Reform*, table 3, p. 19. For his definition of "southern Spain" see the maps, p. 21.

17. Forty-one percent of the area of latifundist Spain was held in blocks of over 250 hectares, but in the six major provinces tabulated by Malefakis, only 8 percent of the cultivated land of all size properties belonged to aristocrats. Evidently nonaristocrats owned a greater proportion of large properties than aristocrats did. (Malefakis, *Agrarian Reform*, tables 3, 16, pp. 19, 70.)

18. Martínez-Alier, *Labourers and Landowners*, pp. 289–94.

19. Malefakis, *Agrarian Reform*, pp. 50–61.

20. In his six major southern provinces, Malefakis found under 0.5 percent of the land belonging to the church (*Agrarian Reform*, p. 67). On the sales, see below.

21. Bartoloné Clavero, *Mayorazgo, propiedad feudal en Castilla (1369–1836)* (Madrid, 1974), pp. 367–70, 381–84.

22. Archives Nationales, Paris, AF IV, 1608^B/2^{II} No. 46.

23. Malefakis, *Agrarian Reform*, p. 83, n. 36.

24. Same source as note 22.

25. Bernal, "Formación y desarrollo de la burguesía agraria," pp. 54, 57–58.

26. Malefakis, *Agrarian Reform*, pp. 84–85.

27. So I conclude from the study of the cadastre of several towns in Jaén province.

28. Bernal, "Formación y desarrollo de la burguesía agraria," pp. 62, 64.

29. Malefakis, *Agrarian Reform*, p. 75.

30. This absorption is described briefly in Antonio Miguel Bernal "La petite noblesse traditionnelle andalouse et son rôle économico-social au milieu du XIXe siècle: (L'exemple des Santillan)," *Mélanges de la Casa de Valazquesz*, 10 (1974), 387–420 (see pp. 405–6).

31. E. A. Wrigley, "The Process of Modernization and the Industrial Revolution in England," *The Journal of Interdisciplinary History* 3 (1972): 225–59. See also Peter Schneider, Jane Schneider, and Edward Hansen, "Modernization and Development: the Role of Regional Elites and Noncorporate Groups in the European Mediterranean," *Comparative Studies in Society and History* 14 (1972): 328–31 and the works cited there.

32. Francisco Tomás y Valiente, *El marco político de la desamortización en España* (Barcelona, 1971), Francisco Simón Segura, *La desamortización española del siglo XIX* (Madrid, 1973), Herr, "Hacia el derrumbe del Antiguo Régimen."

33. Vicens Vives, *Historia de España y América* 5: 84. He cites an unpublished study by Salvador Millet.

34. Ibid.; Malefakis, *Agrarian Reform*, p. 68; Bernal, "Formación y desarrollo de la burguesía agraria," p. 50.

35. Malefakis, *Agrarian Reform*, pp. 68–69; Jorge Nadal Oller, "La economía española, 1829–1931," in Felipe Ruiz Martín et al., *El Banco de España, una historia económica* (Madrid, 1970), p. 392.

36. Martínez-Alier, *Labourers and Landowners*, pp. 290–94; Malefakis, *Agrarian Reform*, p. 69.

37. Calculated on the basis of sources cited in notes 3 and 5.

38. Malefakis, *Agrarian Reform*, p. 69. He finds this a small figure compared to 27 percent for "bourgeois" owners, but in absolute terms the average noble owner may have acquired more than the average "bourgeois" owner.

39. Carr, *Spain*, p. 204.

40. Charles Jago, "The Influence of Debt on the Relations between Crown and Aristocracy in Seventeenth-Century Castile," *Economic History Review* 26 (1973): 218–36.

41. This fact is clear, although we lack accurate figures on noble holdings at the end of the old regime. See note 10 above.

42. Richard Herr, "El significado de la desamortización en España," *Moneda y Crédito*, No. 131 (Dec. 1974), 55–94.

43. See Carr, *Spain*, pp. 274–75; Malefakis, *Agrarian Reform*, pp. 61–63; Gonzalo Anes Álvarez, "La agricultura española desde comienzos del siglo XIX hasta 1868: algunos problemas," in Servicio de Estudios del Banco de España, *Ensayos sobre la economía española a mediados del siglo XIX* (Madrid, 1970), pp. 61–63.

44. Herr, "La vente des propriétés de mainmorte en Espagne," and Herr, "El significado de la desamortización."

45. Based on the records of property transfers in the *partido* of Salamanca, 1798–1808, Archivo Histórico Provincial de Salamanca; Sección Contaduría de Hipotecas, *libros 850–56* (especially the inventory of his property, *libro 855*. fols. 15–102).

46. José Extramiana, "Quelques aspects du désamortissement des biens de l'Église dans la province d'Álava," *Actes du VIᵉ Congrès National des Hispanistes Français de l'Enseignement Supérieur (Annales littéraires de l'Université de Besançon*, No. 126: Besançon, 1970), pp. 129–67 (esp. pp. 143–46, 162); Francisco Simón Segura, *Contribución al estudio de la desamortización en España: la desamortización de Mendizábal, en la provincia de Gerona* (Madrid, 1969), pp. 21–43.

47. As an example of major purchases by urban dwellers in mid-century, see Vicente Camara Urraca and Domingo Sánchez Zurro, "El impacto de los capitales urbanos en la explotación rural: las grandes fincas de los alrededores de Valladolid," *Estudios geográficos* 25 (1964): 535–611 (esp. pp. 548–53).

48. Francisco Simón Segura, "La desamortización de 1855 en la provincia de Ciudad Real," Ministerio de Hacienda, Instituto de Estudios Fiscales, *Hacienda Pública Española* 27 (1974): 87–114 (esp. p. 107); Julio Porres Martín-Cleto, *La desamortización del siglo XIX en Toledo* (Toledo, 1966), p. 416; Alfonso Lazo Díaz, *La desamortización eclesiástica en Sevilla* (Seville, 1970), p. 194.

49. E.g., Bernal, "Formación y desarrollo de la burguesía agraria," pp. 49–50, and in the ensuing general discussion pp. 77–78 (work cited in note 7 above).

50. Simón Segura, *La desamortización española*, p. 297.

51. Anes Álvarez, "La agricultura española desde comienzos del siglo XIX," pp. 256–62; Vicens Vives, *Economic History of Spain*, p. 646.

52. See table of exports in 1913, Vicens Vives, *Historia de España y América* 5: 335.

53. I have developed this point in Richard Herr, "El significadeo de la desamortización en España," pp. 86–94.

54. Salvador de Moxó, *La disolución del régimen señorial en España* (Madrid, 1965), pp. 164–78, 185.

55. Herr, *Eighteenth-Century Revolution in Spain*, pp. 112–14.

56. [Joaquín Costa], *Oligarquía y caciquismo como la forma actual de gobierno en España: urgencia y modo de cambiarla* (Madrid, 1902), p. 611.

57. See the references quoted by Joaquín Costa, e.g., ibid., p. 33. Manuel Tuñon de Lara dates it after 1868 (*La question de la "bourgeoisie" dans le monde hispanique*, p. 86).

58. Work cited in note 56. The author on the title page is La Sección de Ciencias Históricas del Ateneo Científico y Literario de Madrid.

59. Notably Robert Kern, "Spanish Caciquismo, a Classic Model," in Robert

Kern ed., *The Caciques: Oligarchical Politics and the System of Caciquismo in the Luso-Hispanic World* (Albuquerque, 1973), pp. 42–55; and *Revista de Occidente*, no. 127 (Oct. 1973) devoted to caciquismo. Carr, *Spain*, pp. 366–77 is also valuable.

60. Luis Navarro in Costa, *Oligarquía y caciquismo*, pp. 452–53.

61. Nancy A. Rosenblatt, "The Moderado Party in Spain, 1820–1854," PhD diss., University of California, Berkeley, 1965, pp. 106–13.

62. On its permanence through the revolutionary period 1868–75, Costa, *Oligarquía y caciquismo*, p. 17; Kern, "Spanish Caciquismo," pp. 44–45.

63. Thus Gumersindo de Azcárate, Rafael Altamira, and Joaquín Costa, in Costa, *Oligarquía y caciquismo*, pp. 21–22, 198, 624–25.

64. Joaquín Romero Maura, "El caciquismo: tentativa de conceptualización," *Revista de Occidente* 127 (Oct. 1973): 32–33; José Varela Ortega, "Los amigos políticos: funcionamiento del sistema caciquista," ibid., p. 66.

65. Costa, *Oligarquía y caciquismo*, p. 47, quoting *El Imparcial*, Sept. 10, 1881.

66. Conde de Torre Vélez, in Costa, *Oligarquía y caciquismo*, pp. 522–23.

67. Luis Navarro in ibid., p. 451.

68. Sixto Espinosa in ibid., p. 226.

69. Ibid., pp. 228–29.

70. Damián Isern in ibid., pp. 275–76.

71. Romero Maura, "El caciquismo," p. 32.

72. Enrique Fiera in Costa, *Oligarquía y caciquismo*, pp. 509–10. Rafael Altamira and three other professors of the University of Oviedo are also evidently describing Asturias, ibid., pp. 197–206.

73. Kern, "Spanish Caciquismo," p. 49.

74. See Costa's biting description in *Oligarquía y caciquismo*, pp. 50–51.

75. Anonymous letter in ibid., pp. 526–28.

76. Enrique Frera in ibid., pp. 505–6.

77. Richard Herr, *An Historical Essay on Modern Spain* (Berkeley, 1974), pp. 267–76.

78. Romero Maura, "El caciquismo," p. 22.

79. The journalist Granmontagne, quoted in ibid., p. 35.

80. Costa, *Oligarquía y caciquismo*, pp. 80–81.

81. In ibid., pp. 491–92, 427, 379.

82. Pierre Vilar, *La Catalogne dans l'Espagne moderne* (Paris, 1962), 1: 143–58.

83. See Temma Kaplan, "The Social Base of Nineteenth-Century Andalusian Anarchism in Jerez de la Frontera," *Journal of Interdisciplinary History* 6 (1975): 47–70.

84. Bernal, "Formación y desarrollo de la burguesía agraria," p. 63; Martinez-Alier, *Labourers and Landowners*, pp. 290–95; Herr, *Historical Essay*, pp. 246–47.

THEODORE ZELDIN

6 | France

It is almost impossible to talk of the landed interest in France in the nineteenth century. The phrase is an English one and in France it does not apply to a readily identifiable or coherent group of people. The value of including a chapter on France in this collection of essays might therefore be to assist in the definition of the idea by showing what it is not, and by suggesting that the existence of a landed interest should not be taken for granted as natural or inevitable.

In England, the aristocracy and the gentry had for long derived most of their wealth from agriculture; and the fact that they often founded their fortunes, or increased them, or saved themselves from ruin by holding state offices or by participating in industry and trade made no difference to the identification of the ownership of large estates with political domination. In France the landowners did not win political power in the seventeenth century as they did in England; nor did a small group of people succeed in obtaining ownership of the bulk of the land. The dissolution of the monasteries in England allowed land worth as much as the king's whole income to be placed on the open market and to be bought up rapidly, mainly by the rising gentry. By the time the same sort of thing happened in France, with the confiscation of the church's lands by the Revolution of 1789, the people who had the money to buy these up were no longer landed aristocrats, but more often townsmen.

In France, again, the kings of the *ancien régime* had managed to hold on to political power, or at least to more political power, than their counterparts in England, and they had done this partly by playing off the middle class against the aristocracy, selling state offices to save themselves from bankruptcy. Whereas in England the landed interest was able to express itself through parliament and to use the power this gave it to consolidate its claim to speak for the nation, in France it failed to develop any organized unity, and the *parlements*

were assemblies of lawyers, not of landowners. However, these lawyers, of course, also owned land. That is just one of the complications
that confused the French situation before the French Revolution
partly dispossessed the aristocracy and so ended all possible similarities
between the two countries. The landed interest in France therefore
involves adding up a whole lot of ambiguities and of conflicting interests.

Idiosyncrasies of the French Landed Interest

In the nineteenth century the landed interest in France had no natural leaders. In England a relatively small number of families owned,
between them, a considerable part of the soil: in the 1870s roughly one-
half of the United Kingdom was owned by several thousand owners.
In France the situation already in 1789 was that about one-third of the
country was owned by the peasantry, and when the lands of the
nobility and the church were put on the market, the result was that
the country was divided between no less than 3,800,000 proprietors.
The vast majority of these, it is true, each owned very little land. Less
than half of them were able to live off the plots that belonged to them.
France should not be called a country of small peasant proprietors, not
at least if by this it is implied that the land was owned by the peasants
and that most peasants owned some land. This was far from being the
case. There were as many landless laborers and servants on the land as
there were peasants who owned land; only a quarter of the agricultural population were self-sufficient farmers. Even this figure is probably an exaggeration, because among the self-sufficient farmers were a
considerable—but still uncertain—number who were heavily in debt.
The competition to acquire land was such that poor people put most
of their savings into land and borrowed a great deal more so as to
enjoy the prestige of ownership, even though this often brought increased hardship.

A vast number of statistics were accumulated by the government on
landowning, but it is still impossible to say precisely how the land was
distributed between large and small owners. The names of the great
landowners in the country are not known in any way that can be
compared with the list of landowners published in England in the
1870s. It would perhaps be possible to find out who they were, but this
would involve an enormous amount of research in local archives, for
almost every field was registered as a separate unit, the aim being to
note how much taxation it should pay. Another approach to identify-

ing the large landowners is through the study of wills and succession
documents. Here very instructive work is now being done. But until
recently historians have been interested far more in the history of
peasant ownership than in that of large estates. Large landowners have
on the whole escaped the barbed investigations that have been carried
out on every other class of capitalist bogy man. It is known, however,
that they were concentrated in only some regions of France: at the
end of the nineteenth century there were only twelve departments
which had any farms of over 750 acres.[1] Farms in France were classified as large if they were over 100 acres. But there is no ready way of
discovering how many large farms were concentrated under the
ownership of the same individuals: the statistics are about agricultural
tax units more than about landowners. It is clear however that France
had no one like the English or Scottish dukes. To compare with the
80,000 acres owned by the duke of Bedford, one can quote examples
of estates of only about 10,000 acres, such as that owned by the duc de
La Rochefoucauld-Doudeauville; and the pretender to the French
throne himself, the comte de Chambord, was certainly a poorer man
than many an English nobleman. The richest man in France in the
early nineteenth century was probably the duc de Crillon, who left
about ten million francs, roughly £400,000 sterling, a relatively low
figure by English standards, being equivalent to an English landed
estate of about 10,000 acres.[2]

There were several other reasons, apart from the peculiar distribution of ownership, that prevented any clearly defined landed interest
emerging. One was the regional variations of France. Despite the centralization imposed on the country in matters of government, regional
traditions survived very strongly in rural affairs. The fact that France
was politically a nation has obscured the enormous diversity of its
geographical, historical, and social composition. There was almost no
movement in the nineteenth century that was uniformly successful
throughout the country; and in the agricultural world above all, loyalties were local. There was a considerable amount of communal cooperation, more than is usually realized—the idea that the peasant was
exclusively selfish and individualistic is a myth, or at least only half the
truth—but this was compensated for by bitter animosities between
villages, which not infrequently manifested themselves in physical violence, usually in the form of mass fights between their young men.
The sense of being a countryman, as opposed to a townsman, also
certainly existed—that was another excuse young people used to have
a fight—but this was a unity that manifested itself only fitfully and
essentially in the context of precise local situations, that is to say,

where the inhabitants of a particular village had a tradition of despising those of a neighboring town. Usually there were too many pressures both from within rural society and from the outside world to allow the development of any collective or national peasant self-consciousness.

The rural population was also bitterly divided against itself. The distinction between landowner and landless was fundamental, and that, to begin with, divided those who lived by agriculture into two numerically almost equal classes. Then there were infinite gradations among the landowners, and every nuance in these produced keenly felt emotional reactions. Because there were so many landowners, with widely varying incomes, jealousy and rivalry diminished or eliminated any sense of belonging to an elite. The peasant whose plot was so small that he had to go to work on the local nobleman's estate part time, in order to make ends meet, could not consider that he had much in common with the latter, even if they both figured in the statistics as landed proprietors.

The very variety of tenures and arrangements by which the French worked the soil, however, explains why, neither during the French Revolution of 1789 nor in any subsequent revolution, was there any united uprising to expel the large landowners. Too many peasants owned some land to want a general redistribution, by which they were bound to lose in favor of those who were completely landless; and too many peasants had individual arrangements with other landowners to supplement their incomes for them to be willing to risk their livelihoods in a general holocaust. Too many people had won a stake, however small, in the status quo for a land revolution to be possible.

This did not mean that the peasants were conservatives. The idea of a French landed interest standing as an obstacle in the way of progress, or of socialism, or indeed of change in general, is false. It was very far from being a static force. It is sometimes claimed that in certain backward regions, such as Brittany, there was a stable agricultural order that gave the leadership role to the nobles, that in these regions nobles exerted an influence over the rest of the population, either directly through the power they wielded over leases with their tenants and sharecroppers, or indirectly through traditional prestige when they held no such economic power. This would make the Breton nobles something like the English ones. In the nineteenth century, however, this was seldom the reality. It is true that noble landed proprietors were returned to parliament to represent Brittany with a greater regularity than is to be found in most other parts of the country, but this should not mislead us about the extent of their influence. Brittany was a region noted not only for its large number of resident noblemen but also for the great power of the church; and in very many cases it was the backing of the church that was the decisive factor in sending a nobleman to parliament, much more than the fact that he was a land-owner. This becomes even more obvious if we remember that virtu-ally none of these noble members of parliament owned estates large enough to carry their influence beyond a very small section of their constituency.

It also used to be thought that small-scale farming produced repub-licanism and radicalism, while large estates and sharecropping and forest regions favored conservatism. Investigations of this generaliza-tion in a detailed way, however, particularly in the department of the Sarthe, have shown the interplay of much more complex forces. The terms of agricultural leases between landlords and tenants do not seem to have had any significant effect on the influence exerted by the former over the latter. The quality of the land, or the way it was divided up, or the type of farming pursued on it, was not direct indication of the political climate either. Specific areas appear to have passed through periods of prosperity and depression without altering their attitudes towards the social hierarchy. The really decisive factor seems to have been the nature of the competition for landownership. Where peasants were rich they could hope to buy the land; but this situation sometimes occurred in regions that were attractive to local townsmen who wished to invest in the land around them. A hostility was then set up between the peasants and the bourgeoisie, and the peasants would accept the leadership of the nobility because they saw in them allies against the bourgeoisie. This is very different from saying that they were tame upholders of traditional hierarchy.

Another factor underlying the political attitudes was the degree of isolation of a region from other forms of urban interference. Rich peasants could often do without supplementary income from such occupations as weaving or lacemaking. These and similar winter activ-ities placed those peasants who did engage in them in close contact with the town merchants who provided the raw materials and bought the finished goods. Revolutionary ideas were thus often readily trans-mitted from the towns to the peasantry. This is one reason why peas-ants who were part-time artisans were so often radical in politics, while the isolated peasant, whose main contact with the outside world was the local church, accepted the traditional order.

It is important to stress that the division of the rural population in its political and social attitudes was not produced by wealth or poverty as such. Brittany was poor, but that was not why it was conservative; and in any case, it ceased to be so poor as the century advanced. What mattered was how the peasants saw the outside world, whether they thought they had more to gain than to lose from cooperating with it. Bonapartism was an attempt to put the power of the state at the disposal of the peasants, with material improvements, better roads, and higher prices for market produce as the direct benefit; in return the state asked the peasants to abandon their allegiance to the nobility and the church. In many areas the peasants accepted this deal because the financial rewards were too obvious to reject. Where they did, the traditional rural hierarchy was broken up, and the power of the state, the towns, the civil servants, became the focus round which life moved in the future. The destruction of the old order was then completed by the introduction of mass education, which led the young people to emigrate to the towns to obtain jobs requiring less effort and giving more certain rewards than tilling the soil. The state in France was thus very active in spreading the influence of the towns; the state was identified with the urban middle class in a way it was not in England. This requires some explanation, for France was much more of an agricultural country than England. Why did the landed interest not enjoy a dominant position in it?

The Landed Interest and the State

During the Second Empire, the legislative body, elected by universal suffrage and therefore above all by peasants, contained only a minority of landowners. Only 19 percent of its members were primarily landowners, exercising no other profession, though many other members classified under other occupations doubtless owned some land too. In the Third Republic the situation was not much different. In 1889 about 30 percent of the members of the National Assembly were either primarily landowners or else professional or businessmen with sizable landholdings. By 1910 the proportion had fallen to 18 percent, and by 1924 to around 12 percent. Judged by the number of landowners elected, the landed interest clearly received far less representation in politics than the predominance of agriculture in the economy would seem to have warranted. In 1851, 61 percent of the nation was engaged in agriculture; and in 1891, 45 percent still was. Of course, the fact that a rural constituency is represented in parliament by a barrister, for example, does not mean that the interests of agriculture will be neglected. Nevertheless politics was certainly more of an urban than a rural preoccupation; government was the business of townsmen; and the proclamation of universal suffrage was not seized on by the rural majority in order to capture command of the towns.

Here again, however, the situation which emerged was not a simple one. The towns did rule the countryside, generally speaking; the governments and administrators were overwhelmingly men educated in the towns; and the principal tax was the land tax, paid above all by the rural community. Taxes on buildings and nonagricultural income were introduced, but it was only in the twentieth century that the income tax was adopted to spread the burden of taxation more equitably. The reason why this was tolerated lay again in regional rivalries. The land tax was divided up unequally between the eighty-odd territorial departments of France. Exactly how much tax an individual landowner paid depended on where he lived. The struggle for reduced taxation was therefore less to obtain a general reduction than to get a smaller share allocated to one's own department. This was easier to do, because one could argue that one's department was getting poorer or suffering from the effects of floods, emigration, disease, etc. Sectional interests thus competed against each other. Some departments were very successful at this game—the most successful of all being Corsica, which, thanks to the indulgence of Napoleon and the favoritism of his successors, paid far lower taxes than it should have done on any logical basis.

The failure of the landed interest to make itself dominant even in the management of local affairs may be seen also in the composition of the *conseils généraux*, the elected local councils that helped to manage the departments. These councils were never able to obtain very extensive power, and the state-appointed prefect was throughout the century—irrespective of the political regime that prevailed—the more or less omnipotent authority at the local level. In 1840 landowners (who were that and nothing else) formed only 28 percent of the membership of the local councils, and in 1870 about 33 percent. Since political programmes did not play a great part in the elections for these councils, it is easier to see at this level what kind of considerations led the peasants to vote for people who were not of their own kind.

Wealth was one factor, and landowners were not the richest people. At least, a list of the twenty-five richest *conseillers généraux* in 1870 included fourteen bankers and industrialists. This list does not give the income of the bankers Rothschild and Pereire, which the authorities dared not even estimate but which must have placed them at the top; but it shows that Eugene Schneider, owner of the metallurgical industries of Le Creusot, had an income of 1,500,000 francs, almost twice as much as the richest landowner, the duc de La Rochefoucauld-Doudeauville (800,000 francs). The other landowners who figure on this list also had, for the most part, important industrial or financial interests, and though no detailed studies of their families are available to confirm this, it is possible that they got most of their income from sources other than land. The marquis de Talhouet, the marquis de Voguë, and the duc d'Audiffret Pasquier were all industrialists. The leading part played by the nobility in the iron and steel industry is well known. My own researches into the history of another of the families in this list—that of the marquis de Chasseloup-Laubat, who is listed as having an income of 300,000 francs a year, equal to that of Adolphe Fould the banker—have revealed that though he was a notable of a rural area, Marennes near La Rochelle, his landholdings were relatively small. Thus the mere ownership of land on a large scale did not ensure that a man had the right to represent his district in these local councils, as might—just—still be the case in England in the 1870s. Because of the country's political centralization, what counted as much as anything in a candidate was his ability to obtain favors from the central government and from its representative, the prefect. Hence the large number of bankers and former civil servants who were elected.

There were, however, regional variations in the prestige that different qualifications enjoyed. Thus in Normandy and in the large-farm regions around Paris, the prosperous local farmers played a dominant role in the local councils. They shared power much less with bankers and officials, and more with Paris plutocrats who had bought up large estates and so mixed the prestige of money and land. A possible generalization is that in rich areas, such as this one, where farming was profitable and large estates prospered, the landed interest, represented by successful landowners, did win an important place in local government, while in poor regions, particularly in the south of France, professional men—bankers, doctors, notaries—were able to obtain leadership in the local councils. This generalization does not work in Brittany, however, nor in the east.

What made a man a leader in his community was much more than his wealth, the nature of his wealth, his experience in government, or his programme. The modern study of French history, as its focus shifts from the national to the regional and the local, is increasingly stressing the individuality of local units. Two landowners with identical acreages in neighboring villages may have totally different positions, according to the social and economic character of those villages.

Where a landowner lived among a considerable number of independent smallholders, able to keep themselves adequately without having
much to do with him, he might well be kept permanently out of
power. This was likely to be the case particularly in winegrowing
villages, which were noted for their political radicalism. A large landowner employing many of the villagers, however, would be in a very
different position, but then his influence could sometimes be assailed
by an active mayor, backed by a government anxious to destroy traditional influences.

The role of the mayor in breaking up the coherence of the landed
interest was important. The mayor, until 1884, was appointed by the
government, but even after that date he was still the representative of
the government, as well as being the administrator of the village.
Whereas in England the justice of the peace, who was perhaps the
nearest equivalent, was almost always chosen from the ruling class and
in rural areas from among the major landowners, in France personal
and political considerations increasingly counted for more than wealth
and the ownership of land. Orleanists, Bonapartists, and Republicans
successively did their best to raise up a rival against the legitimist
noble in his château, who had once thought of himself as the natural
leader of the village. Residence in the village was not crucial: a son of
the village who was powerful in Paris was not infrequently chosen as
mayor, even if he came home only in vacations; most members of
parliament were mayors of villages or towns. The mayor had to be
willing simultaneously to converse and argue with the administration:
the legitimist nobles, when they opted out of politics, thereby lost
much of their value to their communities, and that was the first step in
their overthrow. Nevertheless, in the west particularly, many noble
landowners continued to be accepted by the government as mayors,
because there seemed to be no alternative to them: it all depended on
how bold the prefect was in his estimate of his ability to challenge the
rural hierarchies.

Summary and Reflections

These are some of the factors that were involved in preventing the
landed interest from establishing itself as the major force in France. It
was only when normal government collapsed that the rural population
took on political importance, filling the vacuum as it were, but seldom
for long. Thus the national assemblies of 1848 and 1871, both following revolutions, brought an unusually large number of aristocratic

landowners suddenly into positions of influence. In 1871 they were for
a few years almost dominant. In 1940, again, the Pétain regime, following the country's military defeat, revived the ideal of an agricultural
France, but the ideal vanished as soon as the normal political forces
recovered from the catastrophe. There was no agricultural party in
the nineteenth century and none of any major importance in the
twentieth century, nothing to compare with the powerful peasant
parties which grew up in some other European countries.

There were not even agricultural trade unions with anything like
mass support. The nobility ran a Society of French Farmers (founded
in 1868) but it was too conservative, too tied to lost causes, to attract
the peasants in any numbers. A rival republican Society for the En-
couragement of Agriculture was set up against it, but this was the
instrument of governmental favoritism and never a genuine association
of peasants with any representative status. In so far as the landed
interest had an organization, this manifested itself in essentially local
meetings, notably of the *comices agricoles*. These attempted to encourage emulation and progress in agricultural methods by offering
prizes and medals. Originally started in 1755, they lapsed during the
Revolution, but were revived after 1830. They were assisted by small
subsidies from the state but even so were only moderately successful
in many areas. The *chambres d'agriculture* that were established by
government decree about 1850 (one for each arrondissement) were
mere paper institutions with no influence.

There was only a sketchy system of agricultural education, so not
only were there few agriculturists with a common theoretical training
but a clear gap existed between the professors of agriculture and the
mass of agriculturists, who ridiculed them as impractical. Four agricultural schools were established between 1822 and 1842. A National
Agronomic Institute (founded in 1849, lapsed in 1852, and revived in
1876) trained the leaders in the profession, who frequently went on to
be professors of agriculture themselves. (There was supposed to be
one professor in each department, to give free public lectures, but the
full complement was not attained.) The surprising fact is that France
established an independent ministry of agriculture only in 1881: until
then land problems were a subordinate or partial interest of the minis-
tries of the interior, commerce, or public works.

Though rural influences were largely excluded from the exercise of
power, the question whether they were nevertheless powerful was

never quite clear. The townsmen complained that the rural population was overrepresented in parliament. We have seen that this was not true if we judge by the number of landowners elected. It was true, however, if we judge by other criteria. All governments feared the revolutionary activities of the towns—and until the end of the nineteenth century towns were nearly always left wing—and the constituencies were so drawn as to reduce the number of members elected to parliament by the towns. Thus even under the Third Republic small arrondissements with only a few thousand electors were given one member, while urban arrondissements with ten times as many inhabitants also had one member. The Senate of the Republic was similarly elected mainly by the rural communes, since every commune, whatever its size, had one vote. In this way, for example, Marseilles, which had nearly a million inhabitants, had only 24 votes in electing its Senator, while the rural communes, with only a quarter of that population, had 313 votes. Nevertheless the landed interest constantly complained that it was discriminated against. Nothing emerged more constantly from it than the lament that it was neglected. This inferiority complex probably lies at the root of the failure of France to produce an organized landed interest.

Farming was not an esteemed occupation; or at least it was esteemed only in romantic poetry. The pastoral idyll was praised, but only by people who preferred to keep well clear of the land themselves. The physiocrats may have argued that the land was the main source of wealth, but in the nineteenth century nobody believed them. Land was very highly valued as an investment; but this was not for financial profit but for relaxation and retirement, for social more than economic reasons. Almost everybody's ambition was to be a landowner, but a small piece of land was usually enough. The price of land was so high that the yield from it was very much lower than what could be obtained by any other form of investment, even state bonds—and it was preferably to state bonds (the *rente*) that people looked for income. There were thus two categories: *le propriétaire* and *le rentier*. To be a *propriétaire* did not necessarily mean that one lived off one's property; the man who lived off a private income called himself rather a *rentier*. The state, rather than the land, was the real guarantor of independence—a fundamental difference from England.

Farming was considered, at least in the early nineteenth century, "the exclusive preserve of the least well to do and the least enlightened portion of the population." Mathieu de Dombasle (1777–1843) was considered an eccentric when he took up farming himself, to prove that agriculture was a career in no way inferior to industry or government service and that it could, if carried on scientifically, produce equal profits.[3] When the revolution of 1830 deprived the aristocracy of state offices, many aristocrats turned to agriculture, and a new interest in farming developed. How many did this is not yet established, but the impression one gets is that it was only a minority who thought that Dombasle was right; most aristocrats probably sought to remake their fortunes in town-based occupations.

The major exception to this was in the north and Paris regions, where large-scale farming prospered on quasi-industrial lines. Because these successful agriculturists came from only one part of France, however, they were unable to become the leaders of a nationwide rural movement; their success only accentuated their difference from the mass of smallholders of the south and center, who were peasants surviving in the traditional way. What developed in the course of the nineteenth century was therefore not a united landed interest but a series of interest groups—like winegrowers and market gardeners—which not only had difficulty in seeing any common interest among themselves but also were often divided internally by regional, religious, and political rivalries. Almost every organization in France in this period was inevitably split on ideological lines, even if these had little to do with the aims of the organization.

The economics of landownership is a neglected field in French nineteenth-century history. There has been quite a lot written on the question of tariff protection, but this has been largely political or legal in character, and landownership as such has attracted very little attention, at least in the postrevolutionary period. There is, for example, nothing to compare with the work that Professors Spring and Thompson have done on England. How French landowners managed their estates still awaits investigation.[4] The gap is due partly to the reluctance of Frenchmen to open their archives to historians, but attitudes in this matter have been changing fast in the last decade. This article will perhaps have served some purpose if it stimulates students to undertake research in what is an almost virgin field.

NOTES

1. Aisne, Bouche-du-Rhône, Cher, Corse, Côte-d'Or, Gironde, Indre, Landes, Loir-et-Cher, Loiret, Nievre, and Var.
2. Adeline Daumard, *Les fortunes française au 19e siècle* (Paris, 1973), pp. 124–25.
3. Anonymous, *Quelques notes sur M. de Dombasle et sur l'influence qu'il a exercé* (Nancy, 1856).
4. Madame Brigette Jeannerey-Joseph's recent *mémoire* on the estates of the marquis d'Andelarre (unpublished, copy in the Sorbonne library) is a pioneering and very instructive work.

BIBLIOGRAPHICAL NOTE

There are two valuable bibliographies which anyone wishing to pursue this subject needs to begin with: Michel Angé-Laribé, *Répertoire bibliographique d'economie rurale* (1953), published as an offprint by the *Bulletin de la Société française d'Economie rurale*, which contains over 2,700 references, and Henri Mendras, *Sociologie rurale* (1962) with some 500 annotated recommendations for reading well beyond the strict limits of sociology. The numerous works of these two specialists are the best starting point for any study. Theodore Zeldin, *France 1848–1945*, vol. 1. *Ambition, Love and Politics* (Oxford, 1973) may be found useful for placing the landed interest in its context; it also contains about 2,000 bibliographical footnotes, both to original sources and to the latest monographs. Amongst the latter, special mention should be made of: A. J. Tudesq, *Les grands notables en France 1840–9* (1964) and idem, *Les conseillers généraux en France au temps de Guizot* (1967); A. Girard, A. Prost, and R. Gossez, *Les conseillers généraux en 1870* (1967); P. Vigier, *Essai sur la répartition de la propriété fon-cière dans la région alpine* (1963); Henri Elhai, *Recherches sur la propriété fon-cière des citadins en Haute Normandie* (1965); P. Barral, *Les agrariens français de Méline à Pisani* (1968); L. Wylie, *Chanzeaux, A Village in Anjou* (Cambridge, Mass., 1966); Paul Bois, *Paysans de l'Ouest: Des structures économiques et sociales aux options politiques depuis l'époque révolutionnaire dans la Sarthe* (Le Mans, 1960); and Suzanne Berger, *Peasants against Politics: Rural Organisation in Brittany 1911–67* (1972). The works of Adeline Daumard, though they are basically about towns, are a valuable statistical source for the relations of town and country. These works, between them, should enable the student to discover what is available and what is being done in this field; but they will also show him that there is plenty of scope for further research. The landed interest, the nobility and the peasantry, have been as neglected for the nineteenth century as they have been favored for the eighteenth.

Notes on Contributors

Jerome Blum is Henry Charles Lea Professor of History at Princeton University. His principal works include *Noble Landowners and Agriculture in Austria, 1815–1848* (1948) and *Lord and Peasant in Russia from the Ninth to the Nineteenth Century* (1961).

Richard Herr is professor of history at the University of California, Berkeley. His principal works include *The Eighteenth Century Revolution in Spain* (1958) and *Tocqueville and the Old Regime* (1962).

David Spring is professor of history at The Johns Hopkins University. He is author of *The English Landed Estate in the Nineteenth Century: Its Administration* (1963).

Fritz Stern is Seth Low Professor of History at Columbia University. His principal works include *The Politics of Cultural Despair* (1961) and *The Failure of Illiberalism* (1972).

F. M. L. Thompson is professor of modern history, University of London, and head of the department of history, Bedford College, University of London. His principal works include *English Landed Society in the Nineteenth Century* (1963) and *Hampstead: Building a Borough, 1650–1964* (1974).

Theodore Zeldin is fellow and senior tutor and dean of St. Antony's College, Oxford. His principal works include *The Political System of Napoleon III* (1958) and *France, 1848–1945* (1973).

Index

143

Library of Congress Cataloging in Publication Data

Main entry under title:

European landed elites in the nineteenth
century.

(The Johns Hopkins symposia in comparative his-
tory; 8)
Includes bibliographical references and index.
1. Nobility—Europe—Addresses, essays, lectures.
2. Power (Social science) I. Spring, David.
II. Series.
HT647.E84   301.44'1   77–4549
ISBN 0–8018–1953–9

Lightning Source UK Ltd.
Milton Keynes UK
UKHW040759100320
360039UK00003BA/63